Protection Spells

The Ultimate Defense Guide against Curses, Psychic Attacks, Demonic Forces, Gossip, along with How You Can Use Wiccan Magick to Protect Yourself, Your Friends and Loved Ones

Your Free Gift (only available for a limited time)

Thanks for getting this book! If you want to learn more about various spirituality topics, then join Mari Silva's community and get a free guided meditation MP3 for awakening your third eye. This guided meditation mp3 is designed to open and strengthen ones third eye so you can experience a higher state of consciousness. Simply visit the link below the image to get started.

https://spiritualityspot.com/meditation

Contents

Introduction

The world can be a treacherous place. If it's not plagues, natural disasters, and wars trying to take us out, it's someone in our immediate circle.

This phenomenon happens more often than we'd care to believe – but we all know the truth: every smiling face is not always friendly. Sometimes, a smile conceals a fathomless void of malevolence, pathological envy, and ill will.

That's when you need to defend yourself.

This book, Protection Spells, is precisely for those unfortunate moments in life. And while many books you'll read about magic presume that the reader is a practitioner, this one does not. This book is for everyone who needs the support of an ultimate defense guide, with instructions in the art of self-defense from curses, psychic attacks, demonic forces, and more.

Here, you'll learn the way of the elemental warrior, standing in the way of unmerited harm and chaos to protect yourself, your friends, and your loved ones.

Because when you're least expecting it, evil can knock on your door. Gossip could be undermining your professional or personal reputation. You may have unwittingly had a curse leveled at you in anger and your wellbeing disturbed by restlessness, or someone may want what you have and will do anything to get it.

With this book, you'll be ready, armed with the powerful spells of protective magic. And you'll learn how to harness the potential of Wiccan Magick to erect an inviolable boundary of protection around you and those you care for.

Because there are more things in heaven and earth than are dreamt of in all our philosophies (to paraphrase Shakespeare's Hamlet), the more you know, the more comfortable and at peace you'll feel in this world. Protection Spells adds a new category of tools to your arsenal, making your visit to this challenging plane a much less terrifying ride.

Wouldn't you rather be at an amusement park than the lip of a boiling volcano? Understanding the power of Wiccan Magick and its matrix of protective practices makes the world your amusement park, and you'll be liberated from the danger of negative influences.

I will share some practical, protective practices that will bring you a sense of empowerment and peace when added to your life.

Chapter One: Introduction to Protection Magic

The first thing to understand about magic (even though this word can be misleading) is that it's everywhere.

The second is that it's accessible to everyone.

You don't need to dress up like Stevie Nicks of the 70s band Fleetwood Mac to work with the magic all around you; You don't need a black cat, a crystal ball, or even a jaunty, black, pointy hat.

All you need is to be human, searching and believing you are the connection between the elements and the divine. This privileged role for humanity is common to every religious belief on earth.

For whatever reason, we've been selected for this role as the mediators of this earthly plane - and the *unseen one*. We can take hold of that and leverage the power of that connection, or we can remain in our untried state. Neither of these choices is for everyone.

But you're here, so you've made your choice. Whether you're an aspiring witch or an uncommitted party, protection magic is a life skill and a new way of seeing the world, which connects you to human traditions all over the world. So, let's start our exploration with a look at popular and world protection magic.

Everywhere and for Everyone

Since the earliest days of humanity, when we got up from all fours and started walking, magic has been part of the human story. It is truly an ancient art form.

The Ancient Greeks practiced Apotropaia, a type of protection magic. While the word is now taken to mean anything you do, wear, or employ to repel evil, ancient practitioners defined Apotropaia as being embodied by an object dedicated to that purpose.

The Ancient Greeks made offerings to the chthonic (of the Underworld) gods of their pantheon to serve this purpose, but the practice of assigning a protective role to an object or deity continues and on a global, popular level.

The "blue eye," typically referred to as the "Turkish eye," is one example of Apotropaia. It's used worldwide, not only in Turkey, and examples of this eye amulet (sometimes called "the nazar") have been found in archaeological sites going back 3500 years BCE.

The "blue eye" of the ancient world was used by the Phoenicians, Egyptians, Greeks, and most of the other cultures in the Mediterranean basin. Its use continues in Arabic, Latin American, Romani, Greek, and Turkish communities in the modern world. The nazar has also found a permanent home in popular culture, living on fashion t-shirts and in a variety of art. Everyone knows the nazar and everyone understands what it symbolizes – the deflection of evil.

Similarly, the "mano corno" is used in Italy. Usually red, the corno depicts a human hand, the pinky and index finger extended, forming horns or *corne*. While it depicts a very rude hand gesture (when made at a man, it means that the man is a wimp and unmanly and that his wife is cheating on him), its use as a talisman is to "give the horns" to demonic influences. The mano corno is also considered to be effective against the *malocchio* – the evil or envious eye.

This talisman is also seen everywhere in Italy, where the popular protection symbol hangs from the rearview mirror of taxis, is fixed to the wall of the local coffee bars or corner stores, or mounted behind cash registers. Naples has its own version in the "cornicello" – a twisted, single horn made of coral, precious metal, or other materials.

The "fico in mano" is yet another type of horn amulet, depicting a medieval hand gesture referencing women's genitalia. Now considered outlandishly rude, this style of the horn/horns is rarely seen.

Just these two examples tell us that the idea of protecting ourselves with talismans and amulets is a popular practice. All over the world and in every possible corner of it, magic is alive, well, and part of the most popular culture.

Apotropaia is one of the most popular expressions of protection magic. Not genuinely considered "magic," the amulets and talismans described are expressions of culture and belonging, tradition, and the ancient societies they sprang from. They're connections to the past and continue to have meaning for millions of people.

Whether all these people or even most believe that their chosen amulet works, the survival of these symbols in such a prominent cultural position is a testament to their power in the consciousness of living cultures. So powerful is the folklore associated with these symbols that people continue to display and wear them. *Maybe they're just hedging their bets.*

But maybe they know what we do – that magic is everywhere and for everyone.

A Whole New World – Things to Keep in Mind

When you're entering a new world, you can't pretend you're at home. International tourists need to keep this in mind. So do you, if you're new to the world of the spirits and spiritual energies that surround us every moment of our lives.

While that world has always been there, now you will be asked to open its front gate to gain admission. That means you're vulnerable. When you open yourself to this world, you attract the interest of spiritual entities who may or may not be friendly, so you must take care. Of course, we'll discuss that as we move through this book, but forewarned is forearmed.

To help underline my point, the next thing we're going to discuss is the Wiccan Rede. This document serves as a guide to moral action for Wiccan practitioners. It will help you understand where you're going and what to do when you get there.

The Wiccan Rede

The statement, "An do ye no harm," is at the core of a poem. (*An ye harm none, do what ye will...*) These timeless words encapsulate the philosophy of Wicca.

But what constitutes harm – unlike the credos of the monotheistic faith systems – is not expressly stated. Rather, it's left to the discretion and interpretation of the practitioner. Situational perspectives may also be applied (judiciously, of course).

Wicca is governed by a moral framework that grants the practitioner considerable latitude but is rooted in knowledge and a loose orthodoxy about using magic within this neo-Pagan religion, based on not harming.

And while Wicca is said to be ancient and is practiced based on older traditions, it is a novelty developed in the 20th century. This is also true of the Wiccan Rede and Credo, which forms a part of Wiccan law, together with the Threefold Law (also referred to as the Rule of Three or the Rule of Return). This law says what goes around comes around. But when the harm or well-done returns, it will be increased by a factor of three.

So, the idea that their consciences guide individuals makes much more sense when linked to this central tenet of Wicca. The Threefold Law guides all Wiccan practice, together with the Rede. These are both included in what's known as the Wiccan Credo.

There's some dispute about the document's origins as a poem, but it dates from the 20th century – no earlier than 1910 and no later than the 1950s. There are many versions of this poem floating around and many interpretations of where it came from.

But the Credo's call to moral, loving action is clear and unmistakable – and rightly held up in testimony to the character of Wiccan practice, which is to "do no harm." And so, the independence of the practitioner, while assured in Wiccan belief, is circumscribed by strong ethical guidance. And here's where you should take note. Wicca's guidelines are there to protect you and those around you.

This book, Protection Spells, is intended to be used by people of goodwill and conscience. The purpose of protection is to prevent the work of evil from having its way with your life.

Be aware that much of what you'll read comes to us from the Wiccan religion, but strict religious criteria don't govern the applications of what you'll learn in this book. Rather, it's governed by your own ethical framework.

Intention Is Everything

Your intention and focus are crucial to the success of casting protection spells. Being in the moment and being present to your power at that moment determines the strength of any given spell.

Protection from mischievous and malevolent spirits or negativity emanating from a known source (or an unknown source) is key to the practice of Wicca, but self-protection and the protection of loved ones and property is something anyone can do with the right approach and attitude.

Protection spells are also referred to as "circle casting." They are only cast for the sake of protecting you and those around you, and your emotions and physical person.

And as this section is entitled – the intention is everything. As you work on casting, your intentions should be part of what you're doing and saying.

So, let's start our exploration of protection with the creation of a physical protection charm.

Onion Braid

This simple charm protects all who live in your home, and what's better than protecting your home and the people who live in it? Why, that would be preparing for food for winter storage, which is part of what the onion braid does!

You'll need onions that still have the greens attached to them and four feet of twine (the heavier, the better).

- Fold the twine in half
- Lay twine on a table or another flat surface
- Place the first onion with the onion at the top and the greens pointing down
- Form a braid with the two lengths of twine (twine is folded in half)
- Do the same with the rest of the onions
- The braid should be tight to hold onions in place
- As you braid, focus on your intention
- Repeat an incantation, depending on what you're protecting (see below). Please note incantations don't need to rhyme. The intention guiding is more important.

To protect your home:

Onions braided I have made,

This charm to hold my dear home safe.

Repel all evil from our way.

As I will it, so mote it be.

To protect a specific person:

Onions have layers

Like the layers of protection for those in this home.

That I create to save them from harm.

Protect and defend (insert name) from evil.

Awareness is the birthplace of intention, so remaining aware of what you're doing and why you're doing it as you say the incantation and braid the onions, be centered in the protective action. As you direct your protective intention to the action and creation of the charm, you infuse the action and materials being used with that intention – this is the true power of protection spells.

What you *will* is what will be.

In our next chapter, we'll talk about discerning when you're the target of spiritual attacks. There are specific signs that you're under attack, and we'll be discussing them in detail.

Chapter Two: Checking the Signs

Did you ever have the feeling that someone was out to get you? And yes, it happens, especially to those who have chosen an esoteric path. That path is full of the unknown, some of which you'll encounter as you explore protection spells and magic consisting of spiritual entities and energies.

While your instincts may be highly developed, knowing the signs accompanying hexing/cursing, evil intent, envy, malevolent spirits, and psychic attacks is an early warning system that will protect you. Psychic attacks may come from anywhere, including those who practice Wicca.

Let's talk about some of the signs that may crop up, telling you that you have an unwanted bumper clinger that you need to be protected from.

But always remember to be realistic – sometimes life is just a weird amusement park ride during which bad things happen to innocent people. Be sure. When we seek reasons for why bad things happen to good people, we rarely receive a satisfactory answer to the question. It's just the way it is. Sometimes crap just happens to people who don't deserve it. That's life!

The Book of Job in the Hebrew Scriptures is the Western locus classicus of theodicy (an explanation for why bad things happen to those who've done nothing to deserve them). If you've read it, you'll see what I mean about satisfactory answers. They really aren't forthcoming, as hard as the author attempts to blame a celestial wager between God and The Devil for the endless woes of Job.

Those most likely to be hexed or cursed are usually in prominent public positions, like politicians or entertainers. People with substantial financial resources are others in immediate danger of negative energies being deliberately pointed at them. Also at risk are those connected to Wiccan communities who have contact with many others (even online). People of exceptional appearance, exceptional talent, high standing in their communities, and those who are well-liked are also potential targets for those of ill intent.

Let's look at some of the signs you've been hexed or are the victim of a spiritual attack. Keep in mind that only one sign is not enough to indicate you have an enemy who is adept at hexing or an offended spirit in the vicinity that's looking for payback. Pay special attention to the quality of the sign. Also, be aware of any circumstances that may have caused these signs to appear attributable to your own actions. Be honest with yourself and recognize when you're building a dome from a seed (mountain out of a molehill). NB: In Chapter Seven, we'll talk about what to do if you believe you've been hexed or cursed.

Injury or Illness with No Apparent Cause

People get hurt all the time. People get sick all the time. But sometimes, an illness or injury that appears to have no cause can signify a hex or curse.

Remember that illness and injury can be warnings about an underlying health issue. Your job is to visit your doctor to determine the cause of whatever's going on. If your doctor (and a second doctor) can't figure out the source of the problem, then you may be under a hex or curse. But as I said earlier, this one sign is not enough to attribute the problem to the ill-intentioned actions of another person.

A Series of Unfortunate Events

A run of bad luck can feel like someone's hexed your life. We've all been there. One thing after another goes bad or wrong in a string of ridiculously bad luck. We throw up our hands and shriek, "Why me?"

You may have noticed that a few things in your life seem to be going wrong. Your car wouldn't start the other day, and this morning, the water was off. Then, you missed the bus (which you had to take because your car was in the shop). When you finally got to work, your boss was mad at you for being late, and the project you've been trying to complete was stalled because the photocopier was being fixed.

Before you attribute your string of rotten luck to a hex, consider your part in any of these unfortunate things. Should you have taken your car into the shop earlier to avoid it packing in? Should you have paid the water bill (is that why the water's out)? Should you have gotten up earlier, knowing you'd be taking the bus at a certain time to arrive at work without being late? Should you already have finished that project?

Rule out your own behavior as the source of your ills before jumping to conclusions. But if you seem to be blameless after an honest examination of the facts, then you may well have a hex or curse on you.

You Have a Beef with a Wiccan/Spell Caster

We humans aren't as smart as we like to think we are. We walk into all kinds of trouble based on our almost global assumption that people are all as well-intentioned as we are. That's especially true in spiritual communities. We don't suspect others on the same spiritual journey we're on.

But Wicca is like any other community of faith – it is riddled with people looking for something the community doesn't stand for. These people are looking for something to heal a broken part of themselves. Often, they're resentful and angry, seeking a scapegoat for their wounds.

If you are in the company of Wiccans or others inclined toward Wicca or casting, then you have hugely increased your chances of encountering one of these broken people. The seekers are not all seeking what we are. They're after something else, and if you appear to be in the way of that, you can get hurt.

Be aware. Listen to your instincts and intuition. Pay attention to people who befriend you too quickly or who veil your eyes with extravagant compliments. Not all Wiccans are mentally or spiritually well.

But all Wiccans and others so attuned can cast a spell. Always remain neutral in energy but alive to the signals people naturally provide you with. Take those signals at face value. They don't lie.

Animal Trouble

It takes a special kind of nasty to mess with the animals of someone you don't like or to hurt random animals as part of a grudge against another person.

But the world has all kinds of remorseless, unempathetic people roaming its wide precincts, and some of them cast spells on the animals of those they target. Here are some of the ways animals can be used or abused by unhealthy practitioners:

• Animals you haven't seen before suddenly being present. Animals you see all the time suddenly being absent. Mysterious illnesses among these animals.

• The continual presence of an unknown animal in your immediate area. You may believe the animal to be a stray or a new addition to the neighborhood, but it lingers around your doorstep. You try to feed it, but it doesn't eat. It just lingers. This might be an animal familiar, spying on you under the direction of a malicious practitioner. Alternatively, it may be sent to unnerve you or to curse you by proxy.

- Your pets falling ill or dying.
- Finding a dead or dying animal at or near your door.

Animals may be cursed to bring misery into your life. Don't forget to include your pets and neighborhood animals in your intentions when casting (when we get there). They need protection, too.

Broken Glass

Pay special attention to broken glass found in the steps of your house or apartment building or on the front grounds of where you live.

Broken glass is a visible sign of a hex or curse and a very old one that goes back hundreds of years. Wicca has many spell casting cousins, and in some of them, potions formulated to curse are broken in these locations deliberately to release the hex or curse on the target.

Omens

There is a plethora of omens native to cultures around the world.

Some omens that are reasonably common include:

- Starling murmurings that occur out of nowhere
- Birds smashing into windows, dying before they hit the ground
- Half a dozen crows lined up on an eave or telephone wire
- A high-pitched wailing sound from no apparent source
- Accidentally breaking a mirror
- Someone pointing at a rainbow

These and so many other occurrences indicate doom in cultures all over the world. If you encounter any strange, unexplained omens accompanying one of the other signs in this chapter, you may well be hexed or cursed or under psychic attack.

Because of the loose-knit communal nature of ideas like omens, we all have our own interpretations, transmitted by culture, tradition, media, art, and the natural world. We are all different, and all our stories are different for that very reason.

That's why it seems to me that Wiccan protection spells are an appropriate point of entry for a novice or the person who seeks a parallel avenue of practice that's not necessarily part of any community of believers. Wicca is rooted in the concept of doing no harm but, at the same time, *doing what you will.* While acknowledging the interconnectedness of the universe and everything in it (which is the fundamental proposition behind "an do ye no harm"), Wicca honors the value of each human intellect and spirit. There are no walls in this house of worship, which is co-creative and co-honoring. Hierarchy is flattened here, and that hierarchy includes people usually forced by faith practitioners to be either "believers" or "non-believers." This divisiveness is not what Wiccans want to create; they are not interested in creating strife with the rest of the world.

They want to be open to a relationship with others as they are open to a relationship with the spirit world and the elements of the natural world. This approach leaves the door of Wicca open for people who take an interest in the empowerment offered by some aspects of Wicca but aren't necessarily committed to the faith itself.

The Navel

I think it's fair to say that a great deal of Wicca concerns not only the intelligence but the general awareness of the practitioner. What is passive worship in some faiths is active in Wicca and democratized by a horizontal structure. What's most important, though, is the similarity between Wiccan and other aboriginally derived alternative faith systems. That similarity is especially evident in the assertion that all is one in terms of humanity and its environment. Humanity is empowered through the elements. But what's remarkable is the individual practitioner's freedom, rooted in individuality and being united in the oneness of everything, which is the center of Wicca.

While one with all that is, a follower is also a unit of the whole and its servant. At the same time, we all seek to create connections with each other. That connection doesn't have a name or a title. It's the navel of the earth from which we were fed on earth, air, water, and fire. In its emphasis on the connection between human beings and their natural surroundings – a connection, which is holistic and interdependent in ways, we don't fully understand – Wicca is a place for people seeking the navel of the earth. Connected again, they long to be fed by the elements from which they were raised, in which they live and to which they will again return.

Remember, as you look for the signs we've discussed in this chapter, you will find in all of them the voice that's been speaking to your heart all along. You're finding in them another avenue for your intellect, your spirit, and your instinct. Wicca cleaves to the elements in a manner that's too strange to accept yet too honest to ignore. In that strangeness and honesty is a mystery to be savored by the respectfully curious seeker.

Chapter Three: Casting a Circle – How and Why

The circle is a universal symbol signifying unity, wholeness, family, community, and harmony.

And the circle is one of the primary symbols of Wicca, its practice, and its ways. The circle is pivotal to Wiccan practice in that no casting work may be done before the circle itself has been cast.

In the case of Wicca, the circle is protection. It's only in creating and working in that circle that you may safely cast protection spells – or any other spells for that matter. So, let's discuss casting the circle, what it means, and how to achieve it.

Why Circles Are Cast

You'll find circles used in neo-Pagan rituals and those of religions like Voudon (Voodoo), Santeria, and Candomblé (Afro-Latin American faiths), which incorporate some Catholic imagery and objects of veneration.

The center of the circle is the place of protection for the practitioner. It creates a barrier which both repels evil and contains the spiritual empowerment of the caster, and it is preparation is crucial because of this protection.

As the circle is cast, your energy is contained, increasing the power of your spells. Your power is, in other words, highly concentrated within the circle. The air around you is infused with your power as the circle rises around you, sloping upward into a point.

This circling creates an energetic cone. As you operate within that cone, your energy increases as you speak and move. That's why the circle is such a key part of the Wiccan way of creating protective magic. That circle not only keeps the bad things out – it keeps the good things in.

Intention Is Everything (Redux)

Intention is vital - it's the backbone of all approaches to those we don't see, like the moving parts of the universe that are invisible to our naked, untrained eyes. These energies and entities are what was being referred to by Shakespeare in Hamlet's "more things on heaven and earth" – what we *can't* see.

The circle is important whether you're a practitioner of the belief systems using them or not. Your energy is human energy and may be directed to the same purposes as anyone else's. What matters most is your intentions. Focus on these before lifting a finger toward casting your circle. Purify and test your intentions to ensure that you're moving into casting with the right motivations and mindset. Cleanse yourself of any bitterness. Turn off your grudges. Your open, purified heart is the wellspring of the casting circle's power. In the circle, you are a co-creator, concentrating your own power within the framework of the elements. That's quite a privileged place to be. Your partnership with the elements is to be revered, held lightly, and with awe. It is a gift that you honor by approaching casting as a profoundly sacred act in which you are not alone.

So, *prepare*. Remember the core creed of Wicca, "an do ye no harm." Open yourself in humility and purify your energies before deploying them in the casting of the circle to ensure your success and safety.

Casting a circle is part of an approach to the realm of those we don't see, and you may imagine this realm in any way you feel comfortable. Your own ancestors may stand in for deities if that's what it takes for you to intellectualize the circle. What is supremely important is the quality of your approach, regardless of your disposition to the supernatural.

A circle is a tool from a psychological standpoint. Casting it is an experience of yourself from a perspective you may not have explored. Self-examination in preparation for circle casting is the portal to humility.

So, you'll need to leave your ego at the door of the circle. While this is most certainly about you, it's not about you alone. It's about those unseen, the elements, and most importantly, those you will be seeking to protect other than yourself. You are not powerful without the fullness of all that is.

Contemplating all these seldom-considered parts of ourselves does not reduce us. Rather, it sweeps the floor of what we don't need, stripping us bare of self-obsession and arrogance. Our will is central, but our will is part of an interconnected whole. In the casting of a circle, you call out; in the power of the circle, you are answered.

So, let's find out how to cast a circle:

Casting a Circle

Here we are, preparing to learn about circle casting, which is exciting! I'm going to break it down for you, starting with the "where" part.

Location

Your circle can be cast about anywhere, whether you prefer to be out in nature or in your apartment living room. Wherever you feel free and secure in your person is the right place to cast. No one can tell you where that is except you.

You need to feel free to call out and to rest with those you've called. You need to feel uninhibited by any possible interference, disruption, or distraction.

Interruptions can be disheartening, but they can also release energies improperly, which can be dangerous to you. There is a spiritual discipline of sorts inherent in the circle, which you'll see as you learn to cast one. That discipline is about energy and how to both gather and release it. Being interrupted creates a spiritual rupture when mid-ritual or when the circle's energies haven't been released with care. So ensuring that you won't be disturbed while casting is *not negotiable* - it's *compulsory.*

Purification

When you've chosen the location of your circle, the next step is to purify it. It doesn't matter whether you're in the woods or in the basement; a tidy, clean, purified location is necessary to honor those you don't see. So, grab the broom or move those branches and other debris to honor the location.

Once the physical details have been taken care of, the spiritual ones follow. The removal of negative or harmful energy is a focused activity demanding that familiar secret source, intention. Use your hands (or wand or broom for practitioners), push all negativity from the location, and concentrate actively on removing these energies to purify the area spiritually.

There's no harm in applying a little patchouli, witch hazel, or sage for the purification. Two drops of any of these oils (spiritual tools you'll read more about shortly) at each point of the area –assuming the shape of a square – aids the process. It's within this square that the circle will be drawn.

Casting the Circle

There are many ways to cast a circle. And in Wicca, there are no hard and fast rules as to how you do it, either physically or imaginary. It's your choice – generally, you will be led to doing it in the way which suits your intention.

Before you begin, bring all ritual items to the center of the circle. Once you have begun casting, you should not leave the circle until the protection spells are concluded. If you plan on making an offering to those unseen as part of your ritual time in the circle, don't forget any objects connected with that offering.

You'll need a surface to be used as an altar. As its purpose is sacred, it should face north. Remember: the circle protects you and your spirituality because the work you're doing connects with the spirit world and everyone in it – even the nasty ones.

The circumference of your circle should approximate your physical height. You may stand and turn clockwise, with one arm extended (holding a wand or broom if a practitioner). Or you can simply mark out your height with a measuring tape; if you feel more comfortable with barriers, you can see.

You can do this by drawing the circle, laying the cord (remember to tie the ends of the cord together once the circle is laid or your cast will not be effective), or sprinkling salt –which protects against evil. If you're an outdoor caster, try using the items found around you – rocks, twigs, leaves – whatever's there. This provides you with your visual representation and honors the natural world.

Honoring the Cardinal Directions

The Cardinal Directions are honored in the protection circle by positioning candles corresponding to each of the four. These represent:

North – the Earth

East – Air

West – Water

South – Fire

Sometimes representative items are used in the place of candles, so if you'd rather do it that way, according to your conception of these elements represented by the cardinal directions, then feel free.

Blessing and Casting the Circle

Your blessing is the beginning of the casting process.

On the inside of the circle, walk around it clockwise, lighting the four candles you've placed as you walk, trail salt behind you to add an additional layer of protection and honor. If you haven't used candles, stop at each cardinal direction point.

The blessing is intended to bless the spirits and others native to each direction. You may say a simple incantation, like, "The spirits of the East/West/North/South I bless and welcome" or "I bless the ancestors who gather in this direction." Say what resonates with you.

Following the blessing of the spirits of each cardinal direction, continue walking the circle for three full revolutions, as you state the circle's purpose; what you're in the circle to do, ritually. This is the casting of the circle.

That purpose is protection, so ask that the circle you're casting be blessed and defended from unwanted attention and interference, negativity, and the will of harmful, mischievous spirits, using the words most meaningful to your specific purpose.

Following the third revolution, your protection circle is cast. You are now free to work whatever ritual magic you require for your purpose, fully protected.

Concluding the Circle

Once you've ended your ritual protective work, you must close the protection circle to disperse the energy that's accumulated within it. To do so, repeat the casting and blessing rituals in reverse, thanking the spirits of each cardinal direction/element as you do. As you've welcomed, so you must bid farewell, with thanks to the spirits for their gracious presence.

Every ritual you perform must be accomplished within the protection circle. This simple process is your security, safety, and spiritual confidence. It has as much psychological significance as it does spiritual, so do yourself a favor – cast that circle before attempting any ritual work.

Our next chapter will explore the world of protective substances and how to use them. For the ease of those new to protection spells and accompanying rituals, I'll be keeping these materials as accessible as possible so that readers can benefit from their purposes and places in ritual.

Chapter Four: Protective Crystals, Herbs, and Oils

Now we've come to the part of the book that delves a little deeper into some of the naturally occurring materials that can help you protect yourself, your home, and others.

Because Wicca is a spiritual practice tied to nature and the elements, it's to be expected that natural elements will be used. Crystals, herbs, and oils are not only natural and readily available; they can be found in all sorts of unexpected places other than online. Remember that many have made Wicca a business, which is enterprising, but there are other (less costly) ways to obtain their wares. Let's turn our attention to these conduits of protection and what they can do for your personal practice.

Please remember that this chapter is not intended to be a comprehensive treatment of the substances we're discussing. We're talking about protection spells in this book, so we'll be looking at items specific to the book's purpose.

All the same, there's quite a lot of ground to cover, even in our circumscribed context, so expect a slightly longer chapter this time around.

Crystals

The iconic scientist Albert Einstein is quoted as having said that "everything is energy, and that's all there is to it." Matter, according to science, is mostly space (Akasha), devoid of what we understand as the material. But the matter is formed in this mysterious creation, bound by molecular structures and, of course, the energy that Einstein mentions above.

So, crystals are "inanimate," but like everything else we see around us, they're *energy*. The differences between the energetic qualities of various substances are as numerous as the substances themselves. But the energy of crystals is stable and immutable.

Human energy, on the other hand, is constantly shifting. It's influenced by people, events, other energetic incursions from those people and events, what we eat, and how we live. The stability of crystals supports the instability of our human energy.

Because of their molecular structure, the stability of crystals is their incredible value to us in protection spells. That stability is power. While humans have their brand of spiritual power, it is extremely mutable, demanding the support of stable energy and the power associated with it.

We will talk about several crucial crystals for protection spells because they're renowned for their protective powers. Let's get to know a little about them.

Black Tourmaline

This crystal is both a protector and a healer.

If you've ever felt that you were under attack from other people's ill will or that your thoughts were unduly negative, this crystal is something you should know about.

Black Tourmaline calms and corrals harmful negative energy. Lately, practitioners are saying they've encountered success with this crystal to protect them against the effect of modern electronic devices, which emit harmful electromagnetic energy.

Black Tourmaline is a powerful stress buster and protective agent. At any time that you feel nervous, disturbed about the presence of someone in your life, or fearful about situations going on around you, this crystal is a grounding influence, bringing you specific protective energy. Keeping it on your person in difficult times is a highly recommended practice.

But this crystal also supports the reduction of fear and its influence on your life. It inspires, and it increases happiness.

Because Black Tourmaline absorbs negative energy, it must be purified regularly. Place your crystal in a bowl of uncooked brown rice, submerging it under the grains. Leave it there for an hour, covered. Then dispose of the rice immediately after you've uncovered the bowl and retrieved the crystal. You may burn it or carefully dispose of it by another means that destroys it, rather than simply packaging the energy to be released elsewhere. Throwing it in the fireplace in a paper bag has a similar effect (no, the negative energy will not survive the fire.)

Amethyst

Amethyst is the "serenity now" crystal. *George Costanza probably could have stopped yelling if he'd had some of this tranquility-inducing crystal at his disposal!*

Amethyst protects the emotions and spirituality of those who employ it. It's also a highly effective remedy for anxiety and thought patterns you can't seem to break out of on your own. Interestingly, the Ancient Greeks believed that Amethyst protected them from becoming drunk!

If you're ready to ascend to a higher level of consciousness, amethyst can help you do it by vanquishing negative energy and the fallout of stress. The presence of this crystal is calming, imparting a sense of tranquility.

Amethyst protects against nightmares when placed near your bed or under your pillow. This crystal also builds your spiritual awareness, which is how your consciousness may ascend, making amethyst an extremely beneficial crystal.

To cleanse this crystal, submerge it in a saltwater bath, leaving it for between several hours to two full days (depending on how intense the energy absorbed by the crystal is).

Obsidian

This sought-after, deep black crystal is created from lava that cools suddenly after being emitted from a volcano – volcanic glass.

Because it absorbs negative and malevolent energy, you should make sure to clean your obsidian often. As you clean an obsidian crystal, picture all the negativity it's protected you from, flowing out of your reality and into the void of negativity. Some people will cleanse this crystal under running water. You can also use the brown rice method described under Black Tourmaline. If you choose brown rice, think of the rice sucking all the negativity out of the crystal, then carefully dispose of it by burning it or otherwise destroying it to destroy the energy. Fire is best.

Obsidian is also helpful to practitioners in helping them discern where negativity energy is entering their immediate domains. Because the crystal absorbs negative energies, protecting you from them, it freely provides energetic clues that you'll have no problem picking upon. It's not going to talk to you (but it *is* ... if you get my drift).

Salt

Salt is probably the best-known and most readily accessible of all crystals used in any neo-Pagan faith. Its history as a natural element used in protection is ancient and universal. How many people do you know who throw salt over their left shoulder when they spill some? Yes, it used to be expensive to buy, so wasting it was frowned upon. But salt has always been of tremendous spiritual value, especially in terms of protection spells.

Salt is even mentioned in the Bible as a measure of value. It's also mentioned as a purifying agent and a symbol of human fidelity and purity of character. The long history of salt as a protective element spans continents and ages.

There is no question that there is much folkloric magic associated with salt. Another belief is that salt spilled at the table is a harbinger of a bitter family feud brewing.

But salt is implicated in many rites of protection. It may be used in reflection spells, which employ a mirror to redirect evil at the person it's emanating from. The mirror is stood in the salt in a small bowl, with the target's name written on a piece of paper reflected in the mirror. Salt may be sprinkled in windowsills and in doorways to prevent the entrance of unhappy or ill-intentioned spirits or negative, nasty energy.

Salt is one of the most common protective crystals and the easiest of all to access and use. And it's one of the most important of the contents of a protection jar. For this purpose, let's talk a little about *black salt*, how to create it, and its place in your protection jar (which we'll discuss shortly).

Black Salt

I'm willing to bet that readers have noticed that two of our crystals for protection are black. Regardless of the bizarre associations of the color black with evil and dirty deeds done dirt cheap, black does not have this significance in the very real world of the elements.

On the contrary, black has powerful protective properties, as we've seen with Black Tourmaline and Obsidian above. Salt is also a powerful protector, but black salt is another level of salt's power due to the protective power of the color black.

Here's what you'll need to create your own black salt at home:

- Sea salt
- Activated charcoal capsules
- Ashes (from sage smudge sticks are best, as these are natural or from naturally derived incense)
- A mortar and pestle to mix the ingredients (frequently found at thrift stores – don't pay more)
- A glass vessel to store the finished product in. (Again, find it at the thrift store or save old jars, as you'll be using a few if you're serious about protection spells.)

If you don't have access to activated charcoal capsules, try another source. Burned wood is the best of all. It's natural, and it's been tempered by fire. Burn your own or scrounge around the embers of the fireplace when no one's looking! Black pepper and the dirt from a graveyard may also be used if you're feeling particularly creative. That said, the ingredients in the list are all you really need.

As you blend the ingredients in the mortar and pestle, focus on blending the ashes and their source with the other ingredients. Your intention is protection, so be intense in your connection with the ashes and what they're doing to that end.

Once the blending's done, store your black salt in an airtight, glass vessel. This part is very important, as any moisture from humidity in the air will solidify your salt. So, make sure that whatever you're using as a vessel is completely airtight.

Once we've gone through herbs and oils, we'll talk about the protection jar, as it incorporates all three elements, including your black salt. Next, we're moving on to protective herbs.

Protective Herbs

Herbs don't just taste great in salads and other foods. Many of them have specific roles in religious rituals of all kinds – from Wicca to Voudon and apothecary spiritual traditions, which combine herbal medicinal wisdom with a ritual component.

As we read with crystals, the natural derivation of herbs already makes them a partner. Their scents and flavors provide us with gifts that transcend even their spiritual purposes. Again, I've chosen three protective herbs (although there are many) which have great significance in the context of this book.

Calendula (A Type of Marigold)

The calendula is a powerful and readily available protective herb. You can find it dried or grow your own to dry. Either way, you'll find that this herb is affordable and readily available.

The calendula has a magic about it that's most popularly expressed in India, where it has a long history of adorning the statues of Hindu gods. Strongly associated with deity and premonitions/prophecy, calendula is a powerful protective herb that doesn't get nearly enough play!

Hanging a garland of calendula flowers at the entrance to your home prevents negative, malicious influences from gaining entrance. Planting them around your home as a flower border is also an excellent protective measure but is only a seasonal solution for many of us.

Sage

Sage is one of the herbs most popularly employed protection herbs. Called a smudge in First Nations spirituality, the sage stick is used to clear negativity, hostility, enmity and evil, and all unwanted energies.

Common sage can be found anywhere or grown at home. Growing sage is extremely easy as it has a life of its own – a highly prolific herb. Do not seek out white sage, as popular demand is taxing this variety of the herb. Trends do not define efficacy, and frankly, white sage is the quinoa of herbs. Leave it be.

Sage will be part of the protection jar we're putting together at the end of this chapter.

Anise

Anise is a powerful protection herb used to ward off ill-intentioned spirits. Readily available and inexpensive, anise can be kept in a pouch and put under your pillow. The leaves of this herb can also accompany you in your protection circle to stop unpleasant spirits from disturbing your rituals.

Placed in your protection circle, the anise leaves on the altar add additional protection from malicious spirits and energies. Anise or aniseed has the aromatic flavor of licorice. This herb is also known to boost psychic ability and attunement to the world of those unseen.

Oils

The use of essential oils has been around for millennia. The Ancient Egyptians were known to grow specific plants to be used as cosmetics, as religious articles, and for preparing corpses for burial. It's from these ancients that the discipline of aromatherapy descends.

Today, essential oils are widely used for many purposes, from relieving stress to stabilizing and increasing focus.

In magical practice, oils take on a different identity. They're often used for anointing the body of the practitioner or blessing instruments used in rituals, like crystals and amulets. Oils are also used to create candles and incense.

In the case of oils for ritual purposes, using synthetic oils is not at all recommended. Using the naturally derived oil honors the union of the natural world and humanity in Wicca and other neo-Pagan applications. While synthetic oils may have a similar scent, they are not derived from actual plants. It's important to keep in mind when talking about oils (made from plants, which are living things and thus, sacred) that natural oil is the one you should always seek to use. Spirits are not fond of the artificial.

Let's look at some of the most important oils used in protection spells.

Clove

Clove is well-known for its curative properties, producing a numbing sensation that helps toothache sufferers. Used as a spice in festive foods, it bears an unmistakable flavor and fragrance.

Clove also has an invigorating effect which heightens the senses. That increased sensitivity serves the work of protection spells well, investing the practitioner with an enhanced ability to test ambient energies.

Used in ritual cleansing, clove also has to purify properties. What can purify cannot entertain the corrupt! This is analogous to clove's ability to prevent interruptions and incursions by malevolent spirits.

Peppermint

Lively and fresh, peppermint is a scent known to promote better concentration and mental clarity. It also promotes renewal.

Peppermint oil's ritual use extends to protection spells. The intensity of the scent of this herb brings the practitioner laser focus in the protection circle, adding to the protective magic already in play with aromatic urgency.

Juniper

The berries of the Juniper plant have powerful protective properties (not to mention being responsible for the liquor, gin). Often used to ward off hexes and curses, the juniper is also employed in its native countries to protect against the evil eye.

Juniper is not difficult to find or even grow. Like the other oils on this list, this oil can be easily created, and here's how.

Make Oils at Home

Whether you have an outdoor garden, a fire escape, or just a table that will bear some pots with soil in them by a window, you can grow any of the plants on this list to create your oils. There is nothing quite so satisfying as watching the natural elements you'll harvest for oils come to fruition. I like to think that growing your own herbs and the base plant for oils infuses them with even greater intention.

But if you're not into it, feel free to source the materials you need – just keep it natural!

Let's make our oil and remember – intention and focus as you create your oil are crucial. Every step you take in creating sacred tools (like oils) must be taken with great intention, understanding that there is a goal that you've been moving toward, which relies on each careful step. The intention is what joins those steps together into a whole, with no step being more important than any other. From purchasing your pots and soil to harvesting them and making your oil, intentionally approaching what you're doing (and why you're doing it) guides the process.

You'll need:

- One, smaller-sized mason jar (because the lid is airtight).
- A second container for the finished oil to be kept in
- A piece of muslin or cheesecloth
- Oil base (again – a natural oil base - jojoba is the longest-lasting, also interfering less with the scent of the herb or herbs you're using - must be used for the sake of your oil's ritual integrity)
- Dried herbs of your choice (your herbs must be dry before you use them because fresh herbs will rot in the oil, and that's a bad thing)

Now, do this:

- Place dried herbs in the mason jar, filling to one-third capacity
- Pour the base oil over the herbs, filling to almost to the top
- Cover the jar and gently agitate
- Store in a dark, cool place for 4 weeks

While those weeks are ticking by:

- Agitate the jar twice every day
- When 4 weeks have elapsed, open the jar, and place the muslin or cheesecloth over the jar's opening. Secure it with an elastic band
- Tip the contents of the mason jar into the other container you've put aside. The herbs will be strained out by cheesecloth or muslin

Every step must be taken with intention, even to the point of choosing where you'll store your oil. Think of how it will help you in your protection work and how it will increase the energy in your ritual circle by infusing it with yet another natural element.

Now, let's conclude this chapter with a discussion about creating a protection jar.

Making a Protection Jar

Protection jars are an ancient means of building a nexus of protection for your home and family. Many elements may be added to protection jars. Everything from herbs spells written out in your handwriting and crystals can be assembled to create a protection jar as individual as you are.

Protection jars are like silent guardians, bearing within them your energetic appeal to the universe and the spirit world. Because your jar is specific to you and because of the autonomy of magical practice, there are no hard and fast rules concerning what goes into a protection jar, except one – intention!

Examples of protections jars have been traced back to the US Civil War period, but the ideas behind them are ancient. Even from a modern, secular standpoint, it's not difficult to identify with the idea that a collection of significant items with known protective properties might be used to defend from exterior evil. When you add your intention, focus, and energetic will to that collection, it takes on the life of those unseen.

Let's find out how to create a protection jar based on some generally accepted guidelines.

Protection jars are great for new beginnings, like moving to a new home or place of business. Creating one for the occasion empowers you to be the spiritual center of the new space and its conscious inhabitant. But any home, anywhere, can benefit from the elemental power of a protection jar, old or new.

While some people bury their protection jars, and while this is a popular modus operandi, it's not entirely necessary. Protection jars and their contents can be sources of power and comfort when kept in a location that transitions from indoors to outdoors, like a window or near a doorway. That said, there is an elemental advantage to burying your protection jar in the ground, where it can draw from the myriad powers of the earth.

Components of Your Jar

One of the classical components of a protection jar is the **sigil**. While we'll talk more about this in a later chapter, the sigil is like a personal, magical autograph, encompassing your energy and your intention for the project – in this case, a protection jar.

The sigil has probably existed from the earliest moments of humanity. Scrawled in dung and the charcoal from firewood on cave walls are examples of personal desires seeking manifestation. Common are scenes depicting abundant prey for food. While the squiggles of our cave-dwelling ancestors may seem crude to our eyes, they are expressive of the key considerations of human living at the time – food and safety.

Written on a piece of paper, the sigil is a potent representative of your consciousness and conscious intention.

A **black candle** may be placed in the jar at the end of the protection jar creation process. This must be done quickly to ensure that the wax is still fresh enough to seal the jar. That's right! Part of the spell you'll use to consecrate your protection jar will be sealing it with the wax of a black candle.

Herbs must also be added to the protection jar, following your intentions. The herbs mentioned earlier in this chapter may be used as they are specific to the jar's purpose.

Of course, **black salt** must be added to the jar. Like the other items, your intentions and spirituality have become part of this tool you've created. Placing a small pouch containing some of the black salt you've made draws on your own spirituality as a source of protective energy.

Amethyst is the crystal most amenable to being part of your protection jar. The crystal needn't be large. It may be tiny, but if cleansed and blessed appropriately, it will protect you, your home, and your loved ones, as this is Amethyst's purpose.

Incense should also be added to your protection jar. Again, ensuring that your incense is naturally derived is essential. Frankincense, with its ancient renown and spiritual properties, is an excellent choice. The incense will be used to cleanse your protection jar of all negative energy.

Copal, a type of incense used in ancient Mayan rituals which continues to be used by the Mayans of the Yucatan peninsula, is another worthy choice. It's probably less difficult to find (and less costly) than natural frankincense. Copal is also an intense purifying agent.

As you can see, the protection jar is not that complex once you have a handle on the items you need and a feeling for what you're doing. As I stated before, you needn't bury it. Keeping your jar in a window allows it to be exposed to the light of the moon and sun, charging it passively.

As you construct your protection jar, infuse each element with your intention and will to unite with those unseen in invoking the favor of the natural world toward your protection.

As you create the jar, what you say matters far less than what is alive in your heart and mind. This is one of the most attractive features of neo-Pagan faith systems. But it's not a license to slovenliness, either. Approach with reverence. Act with reverence. Bring your humility to all the magic you practice.

In our next chapter, we'll move on to protective symbols and sigils, learn their significance and find out a little about how they work.

Chapter Five: Protective Symbols and the Sigil

Symbolism is a powerful, unitive system that unites human beings across cultures. We all recognize certain symbols; the stop sign is only one of many such universally recognized symbols.

Neo-Paganism and Wicca are ripe with a variety of symbols, all with illustrious histories and talismanic powers. Some of these symbols will be familiar to you. Others will be brand new. But as you read about them, keep in mind the power of symbolism. Think about how these representations have arrived in the modern world, almost intact in their traditional meanings.

Of course, cultural overlays and misinterpretations always tend to bring down the party, which is the case with our first protection symbol – the pentacle.

Pentacle

Unfortunately, when many people see the pentacle, they believe it symbolizes the Devil – that's an incorrect belief! While the symbol has been co-opted by groups oriented in the direction of the underworld (in an unhealthy way), the Pentacle is not at all nefarious or representative of evil.

A star with five points, the pentacle (also called a pentagram), is represented within a circle. The points of the star represent the four natural elements and the fifth – spirit.

This symbol is also a powerful protector, and the practitioner can trace it in the air within the protection circle to invoke its power. The pentacle is often used to ward off evil and negative energy, as when it's invoked in this manner.

To draw the pentacle, for the sake of banishing evil energies or spirits, start at the top point, drawing down to the bottom right, then drawing up the left, crossing up to the right, and then down to the left and back up.

For protection, start at the top point but reverse the order, starting instead to the bottom left, completing the pentacle in reverse.

The pentacle symbol represents the earth, as it includes the four elements plus the fifth element of spirit. As such, it is a kind of microcosm, expressing the union of humanity with the natural world (including the unseen aspects of it).

Eye of Horus

Originally found in Egyptian hieroglyphs, the Eye of Horus is a strong symbol of protection and healing. In this context, it represents the right eye of Ra, the sun god.

The Eye of Horus may also be invoked against the evil or envious eye. When worn, it's a powerful talisman against the evil energies of others and against spirits of a similar disposition.

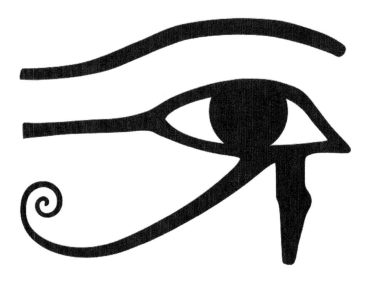

The eye of Horus is always watching and has a counterpart in the Eye of Ra.

Eye of Ra

As the Eye of Horus is the right eye of Ra, the Eye of Ra is the left eye. This side of the pair is most closely associated with being a charm against the evil eye.

Billions of people worldwide believe in the evil eye, which is referenced in Babylonian writings over 5,000 years old. The Eye of Ra can be invoked when a threat comes from an ill-intentioned or malicious person. You can paint the eye on your property to protect it, and those who dwell there; the Eye of Ra or the Eye of Horus may also be worn as an amulet to protect against evil.

Ankh

Like the two eye symbols described above, the Ankh comes down to us from the Ancient Egyptians, for whom it symbolized eternal life. It's also written in The Egyptian Book of Living and Dying as the key to life.

There are varying interpretations of the symbolism represented by the Ankh, but the classical idea is that the loop at the top of the symbol represents the sun rising. The horizontal line in the middle symbolizes the feminine, and the vertical line extending down from the loop symbolizes the masculine. Combined, the Ankh unites the rising sun (as the symbol of Ra) with the humanity of both sexes, representing the source of life and its recipients and stewards.

A symbol of protection, the powerful ideas behind the Ankh make it a sigil of extreme power, not be taken lightly.

Tracing the symbol in the air (like the Pentacle) invokes protection for a sacred space. It may also be worn or drawn as a protective talisman against evil and ill-intent.

These symbols are those most closely associated with Wicca in all its permutations. Ancient and invested with the power of the ages and those who have invoked them throughout history, they are potent symbols of protection.

Next, let's talk about what sigils are (as I've said, the Ankh itself is a Sigil – it was once used as a cartouche in Egyptian hieroglyphics to symbolize the Pharaoh of the day) and how you can create one just for you.

What Is a Sigil?

The sigil is like the spiritual signature of a spirit. It represents the outcome desired from any given ritual being performed.

The word's etymology is rooted in Latin and the Latin "sigillum," which means "seal." The personalized seals of monarchs were also referred to as sigils, as they stood for the signature of the office.

As I mentioned in the previous chapter, sigils have existed since humanity started thinking symbolically (during the Neolithic Age) and scrawling its symbolic thoughts on cave walls. The *reves* (complex symbolic drawings) of Voudon are strongly analogous to the concept of sigils in Wicca. But in Wicca, the practitioner may create his own, unique to his specific ritual purpose.

Austin Osman Spare (1886 – 1956) was an artist with a deep interest in the occult. Spare used a unique method to create a system of sigil creation. He contended that the Medieval creators of sigils, who used sigils to bring forth specific spirits, had it all wrong. Instead, he posited that the "spirits" of the Medieval Age were more like Jung's Archetypes – inhabitants of the human unconscious. He believed that these were the spirits we needed to reach. For those of you who have no interest in the supernatural, this nugget of trivia may help you anchor yourself to the work of protection spells through "sigilization" in the model of Spare. His idea was that sigils could help practitioners address their personal psyches.

If this means of apprehending protection magic serve you, go for it! It's your journey. Others reading will take the traditional approach to sigils, which is also A-OK. There is no dogma to satisfy, so meet the protection spell where you stand.

The intention you take into the protection circle is the source of your sigil and its creation. What you wish to protect yourself or others from and how you're doing it takes the form of a strong and unambiguous intention. With that in mind, let's move on to how you'll create your own sigils derived from your ritual intentions.

Your Personal Sigil

Creating a personal sigil is not just an act of empowerment. It's an act of revelation. In the creation of your sigil, the quality of your intention is uniquely implicated. What you're creating is a visual representation of your will. You are reifying (incarnating) a perceived need for protection again evil energies, intentions, and spirits. And so, you reveal yourself to yourself in sigil creation.

That's why incantations (while they have a place, especially in terms of vocalization, which adds another layer of natural energy to your spells) are less important than the intention behind them.

When you create a personal sigil, you're creating a visual piece of yourself, where you are in that moment. At that moment, your intention is focused on a specific issue or problem. In this case, you're working with the elements and spirits to protect yourself, someone else, your home, or whatever you wish to protect. And so, your connection with the symbol resulting from your contemplations and actions will be invested with the level of intentional energy you invest it with.

And energetic power is the true basis of magic. In your connection to what you're doing, your deepest, most heartfelt unity with it *is the magic*. For these reasons, the sigil is a type of exercise in how the level of intensity you bring to protection spells is the key to their ultimate success. You are the source of energy, uniting, communing, and working for protection. You are energy reaching out to other energy for protection, in *consubstantial* (of the same stuff) unity.

Remember that grand and holy energetic power as we look at creating a personal sigil as a powerful for your protection.

Creating a Sigil

We'll create the sigil derived from your statement of intention for the protection spell you're adding it to.

We included the sigil when we discussed protection jars, so let's say that the sigil we're talking about here is that particular one. This will be the sigil you place in your protection jar! Don't worry if you've sealed it. You are 100% permitted to recharge and revise its contents, repeating the purification ritual and resealing it with black wax as you recite your intention/incantation.

There are many ways to create a personal sigil, but the one most commonly followed is this:

- Write a succinct statement of your intention.
- All vowels in that statement should be crossed out.
- All duplicate letters should be crossed out.
- With the remaining letters, play with their shapes as you think about your statement of intention to create a symbolic shape. The letters are still there, just not in their original order or function in forming words. They're now graphic representations.
- Now, play with that crazy mess some more as you contemplate your intention for the protection spell and why you're casting it. Allow your mind to play with the letters and their shapes. What looks good to you is valid.

And when you're done, you will know.

You will feel that your sigil both resonates and vibrates with you when you've invested it with your intention and passion. The sigil needs that passion for its protective work, and it needs your sincere, intentional energy. The sigil is an emanation of who you are, your energy, power, and spirit. These are what the sigil is truly made of.

Remember that protection is a positive. What you're casting for is a positive outcome. So, keep your language positive. For example, "Keep me safe" instead of "I have enemies." Your focus will have already identified the entity, person, or energy you're seeking protection from. No need to name names as your subconscious and spirit have already done that. And you carry that information in the intention you throw behind the strength of your personal sigil.

Remember – what pleases your eye is the finished product because it's yours.

Next, we will explore using protection spells to keep yourself and your home safe from evil.

Chapter Six: Protecting Yourself and Your Home

Many people no longer feel safe in their own homes, and there are several reasons for this. The world is a dangerous place on every level, including that of the spirit. So, it's time to dive a little deeper into protection spells and how to cast them.

Hopefully, you will now feel prepared to begin thinking about casting your first circle and putting together your protection spell ritual tools. In this chapter, I'll present a series of protection spells for self and home. The following examples cover a wide range of protective needs I'm sure will resonate with you.

Home Energy Reboot

Every new space you inhabit, unless touched by an energetic ritual, carries its own energies. Former occupants leave behind all manner of unwanted things, including vestigial energy. Human beings have their "stuff," and it doesn't all get packed in boxes. Some of that stuff is going to mess with your energetic mojo.

But even if you're not moving, your home needs the occasional energy reboot, no matter how calm the waters may seem. Energy moves around and can be directed at you as easily as it can be generated inside the confines of the home.

So, let's reboot your home's energy!

Marie Kondo Time

Sorry, but she's right about this one – clutter. Clutter is a bad thing. Stuff hanging around your house in aimless piles undermines good energy by introducing chaotic, negative energy. It's a sign of neglect.

But before you reboot your home's energies, it is entirely necessary that you de-clutter. Clear it out. Put it away. Do what you need to do. Give away items you no longer use, mend what you can, throw away what's unsalvageable, and get a fresh start.

Once all that's been addressed, it's time to clean. Everything you use to clean, including cloths, sponges, and cleaning products, should be charged. Hold each item as you infuse it with your intention – the energetic cleansing of your home. You can think of difficult times you've had since the last cleaning – arguments, bounced checks, squabbles - with the intention of cleansing bad energies as you clean.

Keeping It Clean (of Bad Energy)

You will need:

- Sage smudge, or
- Incense (sage, mugwort, cedar)

While contemporary First Nations people continue to use smudge as part of their lives, this technique for cleansing spaces is endemic in aboriginal cultures worldwide, which is where elemental magic was born.

The smudge is a time-honored, quasi-universal method of pushing away unwanted, negative energies and other invasive entities. Made from dried sage, the smudge is bundled together for its specific purpose. Sage's purifying properties are powerful. The smudge is lit at one end and passed before the objects in the space you're cleaning while stating your intention. You may say something like, "This space will be inundated with only my most elevated energy."

But fear not if you can't get your mitts on a sage smudge, use incense made from cedar or mugwort or merely burn the dried plant. You may also cleanse the space by ringing a bell or by dancing. What is done with intention works with your will and that of your elemental and unseen partners.

Once you've thoroughly cleaned the space, you can set a new intention for it, implicating harmony and communicative clarity.

The purification of your space prepares it for its life as a zone of spirituality and as a practitioner's home. This may invite curious or competitive energies, which is why you should always protect your home with some of the symbols and tools we've talked about in this book, including the onion braid you created in Chapter One and the protection jar of Chapter Four.

Manifesting Good Vibes

You'll need:

- A red feather to represent fire
- A protective crystal (obsidian, amethyst, black tourmaline) to represent earth
- A river rock to represent water
- Incense to represent air
- A personal sigil created for this balance ritual, with the intention of manifesting good, positive vibes in the home

Generating and sustaining good vibes in your home is grounded in all five elements, so the materials listed above represent each of the five. You may have other ideas about representative objects. Just remember that each object chosen must be intentionally consecrated to your purpose via the correct cleansing and contemplation.

Create your casting circle as described in Chapter Three and place the elemental representative articles in the circle prior to the purification and casting, as they'll be included in this ritual. Once the circle is cast, each of these articles may be taken to its corresponding cardinal direction, as you speak the associated element's name and request that the benevolent environment of your home is that of the elements in harmony.

You might say, "I honor the grace and harmony of you and your fellows and desire it in my home," or perhaps, "May my home be graced with the sublime vibrations of this circle of divine protection." This ritual will protect you from unhealthy energies but remember – it's not permanent. Those things get around.

The Jewel in the Home-Protection Crown

As I've said throughout this book, there is a huge breadth of practice in neo-Paganism generally and Wicca, particularly, rooted in individual autonomy.

The same is true here when talking about protecting your home. People take a variety of approaches. To conclude the other protection rituals I've mentioned here (which are all steps in the energetic "reboot" of your home), let's seal the deal with a specific protection spell.

Using either plain sea salt or black salt, walk the perimeters of the rooms of your home, trailing salt behind you as you request protection for the room. You might say, "Protect from all evil this sacred place, my home."

You might finish in each room with a strong and resilient statement that the space is yours and that only good will be served there. You might also want to say that you are the master or mistress of the space, without question.

When you're done indoors, go outside and circle the building with the salt, trailing it behind you and speaking away bad energy or entities.

With all these steps done, your home is protected. But always be aware when the balance of energies is shifting and may need correcting with recharging (another cycle of the rituals described above).

Also, be aware of the role of your tools in the mix. These add to your domestic protection when created with the special sauce of laser-focused intention, of course! So, bury your protection jar in the backyard or stick it in a window where it can be charged by the sun and moon. Array yourself with sacred protective stones and herbs and *know this* – that you have created a more energetically healthy and nurturing space to live in.

What about You?

You're the energetic hub of the home front, so what about you? You need to be charged too. And you need to be protected. Part of that involves self-care and monitoring your energy levels when it comes to ritual work (don't get all "spellbound," friends), but let's talk about being alive to the possibility of needing protection yourself. While we're going to talk more about that in terms of spells and specific types of problematic energies in later chapters, right now, I'd like to briefly discuss energetic burnout.

Energetic burnout can come rapidly if you feel under attack. There is no worse feeling in the world and no worse thing that can happen to the energetic hub of the home front, so we're not doing that. Instead, let's talk about protecting yourself from some possible pitfalls.

Obsession with the Work

The world you're entering, as you read, is one that can prove extremely absorbing. As with any system of philosophy or religion, those coming fresh to the system will be voracious, anxious to ingest as much as possible.

That is so normal that we don't even notice that it when it becomes a pitfall. Having immersed ourselves in the work of protection spells and all they entail, we become hungry for knowledge – sometimes insatiable. We forget about things we used to enjoy doing. We sometimes forget to take care of ourselves or other obligations.

This is not healthy, and it matters not whether you're seeking out Wicca as a communal experience or merely interested in the work itself or in those unseen. *Balance is what's healthy in any human life.* When life has too much of one component, it becomes lopsided and often distorted. Be aware of this possibility and be honest with yourself. Your immediate circle may be tired of hearing about this new obsession, which can be alienating.

The solution? Love life. Live it as you always have. Casting is not intended to enslave you or to force changes in your everyday way of living. Casting is intended to enhance your life, making it richer and more empowered. Living more in tune with the fullness of life is the goal.

Neglecting Yourself

Anyone who has encountered a hoarding situation knows what obsession looks like. Obsession is blind. It sees only what it wants to see.

And one of the most common results of energetic burnout is self-neglect.

Who needs clean hair when you're casting, right?

Sorry. Everyone needs clean hair when they're casting. You are entering an ancient and sacred dialogue with the elemental world. Shouldn't part of your intention be presenting yourself respectfully? I would certainly hope so.

Neglecting yourself by not performing your usual self-care rituals honors no one and nothing. Becoming too focused on one area makes you less attentive to ambient energies, less effective in your casting, and (worst of all) less pleasing to those unseen. And you need those entities. You need the energy and wisdom that dwells beyond the veil to be at your best as a practitioner.

So, looking after yourself is not optional. It's part and parcel of what you're doing. Everything you do, remember, is connected to who you are. You are not owned by the work of protection or other spells. That work welcomes you as a partner and a necessary component of the whole.

That's serious business. So, let's show up as ourselves and not shadows of ourselves. Take your rest. Go to the park. Ride a bike. You are an entire world that needs loving care. Honor yourself.

Seek Yourself Elsewhere

Falling in love is an all-consuming activity. There is nothing, it seems, except the object of affection that can hold one's attention for more than a fleeting minute. We all know the feeling. But most of us are also acquainted with the crushing aftermath of a burning love that flames itself out.

When feeling stressed, we may feel we're under attack. Usually, that's not the case. And usually, the answers lie in our way of approaching things. We hold the key, even though we may feel that the problem is external.

Sometimes, love needs to take a breath so we can gain a fresh perspective. Other areas of life that you love – *they need you!* There are other loves and passions outside of that one person, and they all require your attention. Remember that you are a many-faceted individual with myriad needs that require attention and nurturing.

You are spirit, but you are body, too. You're a complex human being with life beyond casting. Do your best to engage with life as you always have, reinvigorated by casting and not oppressed by its demands (which you've imposed on yourself).

You can only be an energetic hub when comfortable in your own skin, happy, well-tended, and well-fed. Loving yourself first is the only way to ensure that you can be that energetic hub for your household.

You are a living partner in the magic that's all around us and for everyone, so love that magic in yourself.

Protection spells and other spells are fascinating and involving, so allow yourself to indulge your new passion with awareness, self-respect, and reverence. *You are part of what you have reverence for.* That should be enough to balance your approach and ensure that you remain a healthy, effective, powerful practitioner.

Consult the five elements with reverence and find in them a model of sacred balance and geometry. That geometry is reflected in the human body, as demonstrated by Leonardo Da Vinci in his Vitruvian Man. Your physical, mental, and spiritual integrity must be reconciled to be one with all that is. Homeostatic balance in the body, mind, and spirit echoes that of the elements and the universe itself.

Should you begin to feel overwhelmed, make sure you protect yourself from negativity – whether external or internal –by saying something like, "I desire the balance and symmetry of the five elements."

Any appeal for balance and regeneration of the positive in your soul is a rite requiring the safety of the protection circle and your contemplative intention. Always remember to recharge your precious self and the energy in which the universe and all its elements and entities delight.

Next, we'll talk about sending hexes and curses packing. The casting world's unfortunate and rather annoying features can be dealt with when you know what you're doing and without upsetting the delicate balance of anything but the silly hex or curse itself.

Chapter Seven: Repelling Hexes and Curses

Hexes and curses are troublesome, annoying things - and as I've said previously, not everyone's hanging onto the back bumper of the spell casting bus for the right reasons. Some folks who take an interest in casting have bones to pick – with lots of people.

And some people just have no behavioral or temperamental regulation. Either way, hexes, and curses are no fun at all, so this chapter addresses how to shut them down.

The Difference between Hexes and Curses

Hexes and curses both emanate from the aggrieved and resentful. Sometimes, people are so aggrieved that they wish you harm, and both these types of maledictions are intended to do just that.

But there are distinct differences between them.

While hexing somehow sounds worse, it's not. A hex is deliberately chanted by a practitioner of spell casting within any kind of framework. But anyone can curse you.

The problem with cursing is that there's no expiration date. That curse can hang over your head until hell freezes over. And that's why the curse is worse by far. *A curse can be carried forward to your offspring and even subsequent generations.*

The word "hex" comes from the German "hexen," which refers to witchcraft/spell casting. Only practitioners can throw hexes, which often enlist the energies and entities of those we don't see.

Hexes are thrown to punish bad behavior (and in most cases done in a fit of bad temper), and the hex's duration is brief. The idea is to send a message, not end someone's life or cause permanent harm. What hexes do is punish with incidents like temporary mental and physical health problems and misfortune.

As for curses, take care with your thoughts and what you mouth when you're angry with someone. You can unwittingly and unknowingly bring terrible misfortune to them. If you're doing that consciously, then shame on you. Curses don't dissipate over time. They linger and destroy people.

Another key difference between hexes and curses is that someone who's hexed will be painfully aware that something has come into their lives and made it difficult. Those who've been cursed may have no awareness of their status, even though they're suffering from cumulative losses in their lives and to their mental and/or physical health. Death is possible with a curse but extremely unlikely with a hex.

Because of these distinctions, we're going to discuss hexes and curses separately.

Getting Out from Under Hexes

The way you go about breaking the power of hexes is, as always, governed by your intention in the matter. When you're ticked off at somebody, breaking out a hex should be placed on the back burner until you've been able to calm down and get an intellectual (as opposed to emotional) handle on the situation. In other words, Don't cast in anger. Always cast in self-possessed humility. Your ability to cast without bringing the heat of the emotional cauldron brewing in you to the matter defines your efficacy.

So, let's talk about some spells which help you break the power of ill-intentioned hexes and curses. Also, don't forget to search yourself, respecting the person you believe to be responsible for the hex or curse. This person is probably someone:

- You've locked horns with, for whatever reason
- Known to you, either in the 3D world or online
- Is probably harboring some jealousy or envy
- Hasn't understood that anger is not the stuff of casting

But you never know. You may bear some of the blame. Before even thinking about breaking the hex, think carefully about any possible wrongdoing on your part. Perceived wrongdoing is not what you're going to examine yourself for. Don't try to psychoanalyze your likely hexer. Instead, ask yourself if your dealings with this person have been fair, honest, and beyond reproach.

If your search reveals that you may have been wrong, reach out. Talk to the person. Apologize. If the hexer is determined to continue with the aggression, calm yourself, unpack your resentment, and move forward. In other words, if you find yourself (in all honesty and humility) to be innocent of any wrongdoing, proceed with your casting.

Here are some of the spells you might want to use to break a hex.

Reflection Spell

You'll need:

- Small mirror.
- Black salt.
- Small bowl.
- An item representing your hexer (or the hexer's full name written on a piece of paper and placed opposite the mirror).

Mirror, mirror on the wall, who's the naughtiest hexer of all? And let's be honest, hexing is naughty. It's mean-spirited in far too many instances. But hexing is not that brand of rage that ruins and (sometimes) ends lives - cursing. It's a toddler's temper tantrum at the mall versus an armed attack on the battlefield.

This spell is an old favorite of mine. I've mentioned it earlier (Chapter Four), but the reflection spell is made to order for the breaking of hexes.

The idea of a mirror used as a casting tool is that evil is reflected in the person projecting it in your direction. Knowing the guilty party with certainty makes this spell extremely effective.

Purify and consecrate your mirror in the manner you've chosen to use consistently (incense is one made with natural sage or another purifying herb, as described in Chapter Four).

Place the mirror in the black salt. Facing it, place the item that represents your naughty hexer (or their full name, written down), like a photograph or a doll that stands for them.

The hex will be reflected at your hexer, and that naughty little imp will have a taste of their own medicine; they will soon get the message that you are not to be trifled with.

Sigils

You'll need:

- Pen
- Paper
- Imagination

And just when you thought sigils couldn't get any more useful, you find out that they can be used to break hexes!

A sigil specifically addressing the hexing party's aggression against you is an effective contemplative spell. Think of the outcome you desire. You want your hexer to lay off. You'll want to create a sigil incorporating that outcome using the same method we discussed in Chapter Five.

Self-Purification Bath

You'll need:

- A tub to bathe in
- Oil made from purifying herb (see Chapter Four – any you've made on your own is best)
- Natural incense (frankincense or copal)
- Candles
- Kenny Gee (*just kidding*)

The idea of bathing to repel a hex is common to multiple cultures and popular folkways worldwide. This practice can be found in neo-Paganism, as well Voudon and its cousins, Candomblé and Santeria.

The purification bath is approached like any other practice in your protection spells tools kit – with reverence and clarity of intention. You are bathing yourself to break a hex that has been leveled at you wrongfully. You are washing off the hex physically while mindfully contemplating the outcome you desire.

The range of herbs and other natural materials used in the purification bath varies wildly, but salt is common in all applications. This is part of any purification bath and plenty of it. Remember that hot water is needed to help diffuse the salt. You may also use black salt on its own or mixed with sea salt.

In some cultures, white flowers are added to the water for their associations with purity. Several drops of purifying oil must, however, be added according to your preference. The space you bathe in should be quiet and dark, with candles lit for illumination. As you bathe in the water, visualize the hex being vanquished and the hexer disempowered and disappointed. Incense should fill the air of your bathing space.

Don't forget to rinse well and contemplatively. Following your bath, you may wish to apply a smudge (or not).

Getting Out from Under Curses

While many previous spells may be cast against curses, there is more to breaking a curse than breaking a hex. While that sounds counterintuitive, who would you believe unpleasant entities would be more likely to abuse than the ignorant?

Because curses are grounded in ignorance, ignorance is what drives a mindless lust for revenge or a burning rage over a perceived slight. While there are knowledgeable people who throw curses, they are not at all well. The kind of hostility required to wish punitive misfortune on others is not the work of a healthy mind. As much as we wish to contain the evil, we can err on the side of our emotional responses to what the curse-throwing party has done. That dilutes rather than augments the quality of your casting.

So, as I said above, *park your hostility and step into your humility.* You are the bigger party, and you are going to prove it.

Remember: When acting ritually against a curse, the malevolence is borne in a disruption of ignorance or mental disturbance. Remembering the reason for the malevolence is helpful as it puts a damper on your resentment. This is not about resentment. This is about protecting yourself from a willful act intended to harm you. Whether the will is sound is not the issue. You have a right to protect yourself, even from those of unsound mind.

While popular culture may claim that curse-breaking is a Herculean feat, I beg to differ. It's not that complex or difficult. It does, however, involve a process, so let's examine it.

Evaluate the Curse

As we discussed in Chapter Two, you need to honestly evaluate what you believe the situation to be or how it could have arisen. For example, have you seen more than one sign, as we discussed? If not, you are not cursed.

If you have seen two or more signs of evil intent, based on those signs, what are your suspicions, and how have you arrived at these suspicions? If this is about a specific situation with a specific person, find out what you can. Read the bones. Read between the lines. Read their Facebook page. Ask around. The more you know, the more successful you'll be at breaking the curse.

Look at the signs you've noticed and ask yourself if you're the only one experiencing these unpleasant indications. Have a word with those closest to you (especially those who may also know the suspected curse thrower). Are they in the same boat as you?

Again, as we discussed in Chapter Two, test your suspicions against your own actions to ensure you're not the cause of the problem. But if you do seem to be correct, the more information you have about the specific curse thrown, the better.

Curse-Busting Spells

Following are some simple spells to break a curse (if you're sure you're under one). Try one or two to see how they affect your situation.

- **Bathing in living water** (river, stream, waterfall, or ocean). As you bathe, your intention is that the curse will be washed away by the power of the element.
- **Bay leaf burning** (sunrise and sunset). As with a sage smudge, the smoke should waft over you, or you may cup your hands and direct the smoke over your body. When the leaf has burned and gone out, scatter the ashes and remnants.
- **Cleansing and purifying your home** (see Chapter Six). When breaking a curse, your cleaning should encompass the whole house or apartment, including the walls and windows. That includes the outdoors - the porch, stairs, driveway - whatever's outside, including your windows.

I'll tell you the truth, none of the above may apply to your curse. You may try everything on this list and still find yourself under the influence of aggressive ill will.

If that's the case, then it's time to pull out the big guns and blow that sucker out of the water!

Aggressive Response Spell

You'll need:

- Sun-charged water (charging water at noon is best)
- Clay that air dries
- Red pen and paper
- Bay leaf
- Black candle
- Container for burning
- Sharp implement for writing in the clay.
- Personal sigil prepared to be inscribed in the clay
- Hammer

To be effective, this spell must be cast at night. If performed at the time of the new moon or the waning moon, you add power, so aim for that (if that situation has not become so dire, and you can't wait to address it).

Center yourself in your intention and desired outcome and maintain these throughout the ritual.

Proceed as we discussed in Chapter Three by ritually cleansing yourself and your circle casting area. Then, anoint yourself with the sun-charged water and light the black candle.

Next, write down what the curse has wrought in your life and those of others – if others have been affected. Make it include every detail. When you're finished, take the bay leaf and fold it into the paper. Now, burn it, ensuring that every scrap of the bay leaf and paper is burned.

Watch the ashes in contemplation until any sign of life from the fire is gone. Set these aside. Now, take a small piece of clay. Anoint this with only a drop of the sun-charged water. Now, add the ashes to the clay. Mix them well.

The clay should now be rolled into a ball and flattened, forming a disc. Make sure this isn't too thin, as you're going to inscribe something on it, which is:

"Be not bound or sullied. Be free."

Holding the disc carefully, inscribed on the other side the personal sigil you created specific to the curse. Now, conclude your circle, blowing out the candle. Take the ritual talisman with you and allow it to dry. The next morning, take it outside early in the morning, leaving it to charge in the sun until noon.

You will now keep the talisman on your person. Its role is to take on the curse's evil energy, deflecting it from you and others affected.

When the next new moon comes, go out after moonrise, and smash the talisman with the hammer. Remember, of course, that this is a ritual, and your intention must be in line with your desired outcome and the steps you've already taken to kill the curse.

Scatter the shards outside, near your home. The curse has been broken.

But you're not finished yet. You must again cleanse yourself and your home of any slight vestigial hostility, fortifying your space with protective spells, as we've discussed in Chapter Four. It's time to recharge items like protection jars. Cleanse crystals. Until you're sure you're in the clear, these rituals should be performed regularly.

And if you can't break the curse, remember – it could be a problem you need to solve in yourself and not an external problem. If that's not the case, consult with someone who has extensive experience in breaking curses.

Hold onto your hats because we're just getting started... Next, we're going to talk about protecting yourself by deflecting psychic attacks.

Chapter Eight: Deflecting Psychic Attacks

A psychic attack isn't necessarily about ghosts trying to take over your brain. It's much more about energies and people who direct those energies toward you. Their reasons for doing so aren't mysterious – envy, jealousy, competitiveness, resentment, and other sophomoric reasons are unfortunate drivers in many cases.

So, let's start by clarifying what psychic attacks can feel like and how they might manifest in your life.

The Whats and Whys of Psychic Attacks

A physical attack is easy to define because it's visible and usually felt on a physical level. Psychic attacks are more nebulous and less easy to pinpoint.

The evil eye is a nexus, a central point, between the psychic and the physical attack because you can both feel and see it. You can detect the evil gleam in the eye of one who wishes you ill. But a psychic attack might also come in the form of people who suck your energy away with negativity and self-pity. While they may not mean it "in that way," ambient energies pick up on the negativity and coalesce around it, giving it life. This is a good reason to avoid people who leave you feeling depleted after you've interacted with them. It's not just their neediness; it's their demand that their neediness is more important than your mood, both in that moment and later. The needy person who clings to you seeking attention, financial and emotional support, and a constant listening ear is attacking you psychically just as surely as the person giving you the evil eye.

Resentment, envy, and jealousy join negativity as emotional frameworks best left to their own devices. Once you've seen the red flag, don't ignore it. People who bear these emotional frameworks in your confrontation may not believe they mean you harm, but they do. Their resentment, envy, and jealousy are just as corrosive as the bottomless pit of neediness. All these emotions drain you spiritually, emotionally, and eventually, physically.

A psychic attack can be unwitting, certainly; The needy person, attached to you like a mosquito drawing blood to feed itself, is not concerned with your wellbeing. That needy person is concerned with sustaining themself. The narcissism of neediness is in its impacts on those who must feed the needy beast.

But when it comes to resentment, envy, and jealousy, those whose emotional frameworks are geared to you in this way are easily led into fleeting thoughts of annihilation. When people feel you have something they want and deserve more than you do, these thoughts may arise. When you draw people to you with your grace, beauty, poise, and intellect, you are also in the sight of those in the grip of these unhealthy emotions. And when the emotion at work is jealousy, the price you pay from the resulting curse can be catastrophic.

Curses are born in the burdens of the mind and loosed out of the mouth. But even if the attacker's mouth isn't open to let the thought become words, the thought itself, boiling in the attacker's head, is enough.

The energy of emotions like resentment, envy, and jealousy is *fiery and destructive*. And this is not the purifying fire of ritual; this is the fire that burns eternally in the depths of Hades. It is a fire generated by emotions that have not been tempered by reason. They're dangerous, permeating every cell of the attacker's being. The emotions we're talking about are epic and cinematic. They're not sweet little hiccups in the calm surface of the persona. These emotions can consume people with obsessive thoughts and angry, mutilated ideation directed at the innocent.

That's a lot of negative energy, and when it hits you, you'll feel it.

The Energy Vampires

The vampire in popular culture is an ancient icon of blood-sucking terror. But those vampires, unlike the ones we're about to discuss, feed on blood.

Energy vampires feed on your energy. They do this by forever calling on your willingly listening ear, your unending compassion, your great advice. They talk about how difficult everything is for them and how they're always the victims of circumstance, other people, life itself. They are blameless. It's always someone else's fault, never the energy vampires' fault.

We all know someone like this. Whether we admit it or not, some of the people around us are trying to fill a profound void in themselves by sucking the energy out of others. Sometimes they're aware they're doing it. Mostly, though, these people are unconscious drains on your goodwill and patience – and in another plane could be called *narcissistic*.

With energy vampires, nothing is a two-way street. Everything is about them. You may have a problem you want to discuss with your energy vampire. You sit down over coffee, and as you tell the vampire your tale of the woe, your tale strangely morphs into a story about the vampire and the vampire's endless challenges.

And the vampire always has challenges – and drama. Drama is their color, and there's always plenty of it to wrap themselves in, ever so pathetically. And no matter what, that drama features the vampire as the longsuffering victim, even though they are frequently the heroes of every story they tell you. They're the hero when they're trying to impress upon you how worthy they are, and the victim when they need your shoulder to soak with their bitter, endless tears.

But don't interrupt! That's when the energy vampire will guilt you into listening for another couple of hours. And if you dare suggest that the vampire might need a professional listening ear, you will be told to never insult them like that again! They're just a normal person under attack from everyone they run across. *Everyone!*

Some people – a lot of people – have a problem with creating strong boundaries. When we come across these people, it's not hard to draw boundaries if we're aware and know how to draw them effectively. But the real problem arises when the energy vampire in question has determined that it's your energy they're most interested in and is determined to drain.

This is the type of energy vampire that you need to beware of. There is most likely a strong element of narcissistic pathology involved, as energy vampires like this have an agenda, and it is to feed off your energy.

Your garden variety energy vampire can be dealt with by erecting boundaries and socially distancing yourself to whatever degree feels right to avoid that drained, exhausted feeling you have after interacting with them. But it's an intentional, practiced energy vampire you're dealing with, that's a horse of a different color. With these people, the only way to deal with them is to cease all contact.

Most importantly, do not make, much less sustain, eye contact with this type of energy vampire. They rely on it to draw energy from you. Do not visualize or think about the energy vampire (unless casting to deflect a psychic attack initiated by them).

I'm quite passionate about this type of disordered person because I've had up-close and personal encounters with several of them. Let me tell you the story. It's not pretty, but at least it has a happy ending – which is, of course, a protection spell.

Nosferatu Calling

Nosferatu (the Queen of the Damned and thus, of all vampires) unremarkably came into my life one day. I was quietly visiting with friends at a corner coffee shop. We all met there frequently. There was nothing about her to suggest there was anything wrong.

But as time went by, I began to sense the energy around this person. For one, she didn't acknowledge me or any of my friends. She chattered animatedly with the men present. Women were ignored. She would go as far as to turn her back when a woman came in, although (over time), she began waving to everyone who came in the door as though she owned the place.

I watched and listened. I did not engage. More time went by. On the days I went in to meet my friends, I noticed a strange silence when I walked through the front door. Everyone acted normally, but there was almost a question hanging in the air – something like, "Is she one of us?" Increasingly, the answer came back "no."

But then, one day, after weeks on end of witnessing this woman's deep freeze towards us, I walked in alone – to the usual odd silence – and sat down. Nosferatu approached me, coffee cup in hand.

Sitting down without even asking, Nosferatu launched into an introduction, which I received warily. Returning the niceties, I thought she might sit and perhaps get to know me, but she didn't. She got up and walked back to her seat. That was the last time she ever spoke to me.

Yes, it was strange. But over the following months, things were to become much stranger. Rumors began to circulate, and suddenly, I found myself in the center of a "catfight" that I didn't even know I was involved in.

Nosferatu had decided that I was involved.

At the same time, strange things began to happen. I experienced numbness in my legs. One day, it was so bad, I had to stop, lean against something, and let it pass. I had problems with my bank. I lost work. I lost friends.

Nosferatu had done what she does to many unwitting people – she had deliberately started to drain my energy. The rumors all concerned my hatred of her and my jealousy. The truth was that I simply considered Nosferatu's behavior in the presence of other women odd. I didn't even know her, much less care what she thought of me. There were no emotions involved on my end. But there were from hers. It seemed to me that Nosferatu wanted to be "the only girl" in the coffee shop.

Putting two and two together and having had enough of Nosferatu's internalized misogyny, I continued visiting with my friends as I always had. The attacks also continued. Then my friends started telling me they'd been having physical problems and were feeling abnormally tired. They had all been approached by Nosferatu, but also one-on-one when the rest of us weren't present.

And this is a key point – do not allow yourself to engage alone with energy vampires of the Nosferatu variety. Always be aware when these people are present and if you're alone, keep moving. Don't allow the vampire to make eye contact or come anywhere near you.

So, here's what I did about Nosferatu.

Psychic Shielding

In my situation, it was clear that Nosferatu was directly attacking both my friends and me by various means. She had drawn near me, not to get to know me but to suck energy from me, using eye contact. But that was not enough; she had also attempted to spread negativity by word of mouth. I had a strong bad feeling that Nosferatu was channeling her nasty energy in other ways – magical ways. So, my best course of action was to shield myself from further abuse. I explained to my friends what I planned to do. They know me well and, like me, are energy workers and casters.

Of course, my solution was the bubble shield, a strategy my friends agreed sounded like the best course of action. We all created psychic bubble shields, forming around ourselves a sphere of protection from the vampiric incursions of Nosferatu.

The bubble shield is a method of psychic shielding and is widely considered the most effective means of preventing unwanted vampiric activity and the incursion of unhealthy energies and entities.

You have an interest in protection spells. You may even have an academic interest in the supernatural, but that interest comes with baggage. Those who peer into the mysteries of elemental magic may see others looking back. These energies and entities aren't necessarily bad, but they're not all sunshine and unicorns either. Your interest, whatever it's based on, attracts a commensurate spiritual interest from other quarters.

And so, the bubble shield is a means of psychic protection against the envious, ill-intentioned, and ill-willed, like Nosferatu. I suspect that Nosferatu is an interested party herself, but one unacquainted with the backbone of Wicca, "an do ye no harm." She is most probably a rogue who has gone well off-road or was never on the road, to begin with. I chose the bubble shield for psychic protection from her due to this specific factor. She's an ill-willed dabbler with abundant bad energy shooting out of her. That's just bad for everyone, including her. Nosferatu is basically an annoyance, though. She's messing with the wrong women, and while she may have picked up a chop or two to compliment her inner darkness, she is too rooted in her own demons to be truly effective. The bubble shield was a defensive action that made it clear to her that we would remain unaffected by her aggressions, large and small, direct and indirect.

And - they subsided - because people like Nosferatu need an audience, and we were not it. We were altogether too boringly oblivious to her energetic greatness for her to bother with. When you feel protected, you feel confident and in control.

Even if there's no Nosferatu in your life, you're well-served in protecting yourself, so here's how to do just that with the bubble shield.

Creating a Psychic Bubble Shield

Of all the psychic shielding techniques, this one is the simplest. This minor spell is relatively easy but still delivers what you need – protection. A lot of that protection, as you know, comes from your intention in preparing it. But add to that the confidence you've invested and have within you in taking the situation by the horns and putting it in its place.

It is truly satisfying to know that you've done that, as well as having boosted your self-esteem, refusing to fall prey to self-pity or self-recrimination. By taking steps to protect yourself from psychic attacks, you become their master. You become aware of them, and you learn, over time, what to do about them. The bubble shield is a good start.

Cast your circle and get ready to build one!

My preferred method for creating a bubble shield is to ground it with a specific intention. In my case, that was, "Step off, Nosferatu!"

For you, it might be, "This private sphere is free of all negative energies and incursions of those who employ them." Your intention and wish are for a creative, personal methodology of creating a bubbling sphere and having that bubble shield psychically shield you from all and any attacks.

As you focus on the bubble rising from the foundation of your intention, you are gathering energy. Visualize the bubble forming around you as you repeat your intention. Continue doing this focus work to bring to life the most enduring and effective bubble shield.

Remember to visualize your bubble to keep your intention for the shield's purpose central to your contemplative work. Visualize the way it looks while weaving its purpose into that visualization as words, moving pictures, symbols – whatever evokes the function of the bubble most fully to you.

This work can be done outside the circle. *Who am I to say it shouldn't be?* But I will say this – the cumulative energy of the circle contributes to the energy available to you in creating a bubble shield. Psychic shields are spells, and spells require your energy and focused intention to be effective. The casting circle's intent is protection but within that protective circle is your most profound power. Especially when you're new to casting, the protection circle focuses your intentions toward the spiritual and sacred. For me, the circle is an incredibly useful tool for beginning casters for these reasons.

And when you're creating a bubble shield to protect yourself from the ill-intentioned, power is what you need. You also need confidence, and while the bubble shield is a self-empowering action in which you stand up for yourself, the circle provides an accumulation of power and spiritual significance, which adds to your conviction as you cast.

As you move along in your protection spells journey, you'll grow in strength and confidence, but you'll find that this simple protection spell will invest you with the confidence not just to defend yourself but to be formidable and ethically sound while you're doing it.

Next, we'll talk about banning evil forces, entities, and the other hooligans of the unseen world.

Chapter Nine: Banishing Evil Forces

Not everything in the unseen world is friendly. Not all those we cannot see are our friends. Some of those entities and energies are and can be totally unwholesome, bringing with them chaos and malice.

We've all read the stories and seen the films. We've seen Hollywood's representations of demonic possession, angels, demons, the Illuminati, and various witchy kitschy attempts at penetrating the elemental mysteries.

But we need to discuss this part of the world unseen, as ignoring it can make for some unfortunate surprises. And nobody likes those.

In this chapter, we'll talk about the forces around us that make the hairs on the backs of our necks and arms stand on end, making the cat hiss and the dog whine. The wind howls a little louder in their presence, and the night takes on a deeper mantle of velvet, impenetrable darkness.

Let's explore the world of demons, evil spirits, and hostile entities and find out how to manage their presence safely.

Not Fun Guys

Unless you're Hitler or someone equally psychopathic, the evil forces we're talking about are nobody's idea of a good time or good mates.

To start, evil spirits and demons are essentially the same things. While I'm sure the world is brimming with complex demonologies that might provide a hierarchy to energies that really don't need that kind of encouragement, demons are evil spirits and vice versa. These are not the dearly departed, sufficiently aggrieved to hang around. *(Those guys aren't evil; they're sad. They just aren't ready to move on.)* Evil spirits/demons have never been as we are now. They are permanent thorns on the world's side. They are beings in spirit only.

As I said above, the world is brimming with complex demonologies, accounts of demons, and demons who were once angels. But we're not here to talk about apocryphal sources in world religions (and you'll find angels in demons in many, if not most of them). We're here to talk about evil spirits.

Richard Gallagher is an American psychologist who works with Roman Catholic priests. Gallagher believes in evil forces – evil spirits or demons.

So, if you think that the whole idea of evil spirits is just a load of mumbo jumbo, Dr. Gallagher begs to differ; he's seen some things. And while he believes that demon possession is rare, he also believes it exists because he could not otherwise explain the mid-exorcism levitation he witnessed, among many other phenomena which could not be explained.

And Gallagher is not alone. M. Scott Peck is a psychiatrist who set out to disprove demon possession but wound up, after extended explorations and observations, seeing with his own eyes that there was no other explanation but demon possession in certain cases which couldn't be explained by science. He has written two books on the subject.

In a wide variety of organized, traditional religious systems, the concept of demons is often juxtaposed against angels. This type of conception has evolved to include complex hierarchies of both types of entities – but that has more to do with the anxious human need to create categories and rankings, with labels attached, providing a superficial sense of control. Demons also appear in neo-Pagan and aboriginal spiritual constructs, meaning that the religious and popular conceptions of the demon may have originally sprung from the human fear of death. In some cultures, representations of the dead point to a wavering line between ancestor worship and demonology.

But evil spirits are not subject to tidy compartmentalization. These are supernatural entities, never incarnate as we are, yet boasting a will and consciousness. Demons are all around us, powerless to intervene, except in certain circumstances. While demon possession, as discussed above, is a common theme in popular culture, Gallagher and Peck agree that these events are rare.

Demonic incursions into the physical world are misunderstood and seldom spoken about. While some believe in the power of evil spirits as strongly as they do in angels, they know little of how these entities operate. But when intellectuals and ostensibly secularly minded people like psychologists and psychiatrists encounter this dark world in the course of their work and talk about it, we should understand that as a *big deal*. And we should take the existence of these ethereal spirits seriously.

In Wicca, evil spirits or demons aren't included when seeking counsel and guidance from the spirits, but they are acknowledged as being part of the natural order as "negative energies." But these energies, having the human attributes of consciousness and will, do not have the rest of humanity's virtues - like compassion, empathy, love, and equanimity. Demons are offended by this. They're also offended by the fact that we are creatures with bodies – something else they don't have. While some claim that demons are fallen angels,

I tend to think they were once aspiring angels, shown the door before even getting near a pair of wings. They're that petty and jealous.

That's why demons like to jump into human bodies. It's only in the human body that the demon experiences the fullness of the human experience.

And it's only in the human body that the demon can completely despoil and, if left unchecked, destroy that same body.

But why? Because it is the human body and all, it contains – the brain and nerves and muscle and bone and miraculous instinct informed by blessed reason – that the demon most desires and envies above all else. There is nothing so enticing to the evil spirit than the destruction of what it can never have – humanity.

How to Banish Them

For the types of spirits we're discussing, there are no half measures. For that reason, we'll be calling on the Greek goddess, Hecate, for her intervention.

Hecate is the goddess of the night, the underworld, and witchcraft. But that's not all; Hecate is a badass, ruling over the soul of the world and a soter (savior) goddess.

That's a lot of influence and the reason contemporary practitioners turn to her in times of crisis, like an incursion of evil spirits or entities. *This is not greasy kid stuff.*

For our purposes, you should know that Hecate is also the goddess of transitions, meaning she is there at the boundary between life and death, the world we know and that of the spirits – those unseen. These entities pass back and forth between the worlds, so when Hecate is made aware of troublemakers, she is in a position to assist.

Hecate is also known as a "triple goddess," invested with the ability to see the past, future, and present simultaneously. So, fear not, dear ones – Hecate has your back, and she's a 360-degree vision goddess, at that.

Because of her status as a goddess of transitions, Hecate has a special kinship with dogs. This kinship relates to the role of Cerberus, who guards the entrance to the underworld in Greek mythology. Hecate is also associated with garlic.

Most of us know that garlic is almost universally used as a talisman against evil and the forces who bear it into the world. We usually associate this usage as that employed to repel vampires. But Hecate is also a great friend of garlic's talismanic powers.

Invoking Hecate

You'll need:

- Three sewing needles.
- 1 head of garlic
- A y-shaped crossroads (yes – you will be performing your ritual there, so be sure it's quiet and that you won't be disturbed)
- A new moon – a new moon is the best time to invoke Hecate - at night

Your intentions must be pure. Do not call on Hecate to settle a score or with any ill intentions. Cleanse yourself by bathing in salt or purifying with incense or sage, all the while contemplating what you're about to do and who you're going to invoke.

Cast your circle (this is non-negotiable in this instance – I consider it a necessity for all spells, especially for novice casters, but when you're calling on Hecate, the circle is necessary).

Once the circle is cast and your power is concentrated within it, bless your needles with incense or by whatever method you prefer. Dedicate one to Hecate.

You might want to say something like, "Great and good goddess, Hecate, I am in need of you. Hold me in your eternal embrace as you help me push away the evil forces being lined up against me by _____ away." (If you know the name of someone doing this, say it – if not, stop at "against me away.")

Now, pierce the head of garlic with the needle you've dedicated to Hecate. As you pierce the garlic with the second needle, you may repeat the same invocation or allow your own words to rise within you. Repeat this process with the third needle. The needles should be arranged around the top edge of the garlic as it sits on the altar in front of you.

Now say, "Great and good goddess Hecate, this garlic I have offered as a talisman of healing and protection. It is my tribute to you for your divine assistance, guidance, and loving care for me."

Following your formal praise of the goddess for her assistance, your spell is cast. The needles should be removed from the garlic and disposed of carefully, as they are now invested with the evil that has been plaguing you. The garlic should be burned completely.

Evil is all around us, breaking into our world out of hatred, jealousy, and malicious envy. It is carried in people and operates through the spirits' malevolent usage of them. When these forces become apparent to you (see Chapter Two), call on Hecate's ancient, divine intervention.

To Remove and Prevent Vestigial Negative Energies

Vestigial energy is like a negativity hangover. It clings to you sometimes and to your home – or both. But it's simple enough to keep that energy at bay with some help from your arsenal of casting tools.

One of these is **cedar oil**. This oil is a powerful cleanser, and placing a drop in the corner of each room as you ask that vestigial energy from the evil forces you have banished be cleansed. A drop in your bathwater is another measure you can take, making the same request.

Adding **salt** to your negative energy cleansing bath is also called for. The salt bath can be done regularly to ensure that your personal energy remains balanced and without blemish (see Chapter 12).

And never rule out your own energy as bringing about negativity. No one is to blame for that, so it's no reason to beat yourself up. But being aware and make sure your energetic output is healthy. The human world responds as the spirit world does to negative energy. Those responses are different, of course. Humans don't like it much – *evil spirits feed off it.* That said, positive energy can be just as attractive to these disordered spirits if they've been invoked to attack you. Disordered people often have a similar response to positive energy. They loathe it because they don't have it. Strange that - disordered people and disordered spirits are so similar in temperament. But then, everything is connected and "as above, so below" (or wherever the world of the spirits is).

Always seek to maintain an energy that is all you and tempered by understanding those we don't see. Regular salt baths can be enormously helpful in this respect. Keeping your energy grounded and centered in your practice and contemplation of it is a project of psychological self-care, and we all need some of that in our lives.

Of course, a **sage smudge** of yourself and your home is never a bad idea, especially when you've recently banished unsavory and unwelcome guests. Sage is everyone's favorite energetic cleanser. There's a reason it's considered sacred in so many diverse cultures.

Like evil forces, gossip and slander are born in the intentions of human beings. But their chattering can be stilled. In our next chapter, we'll find out how.

Chapter Ten: Stopping Gossip and Slander

People's tongues do love to wag. Sometimes, it's almost as though they can't help themselves. They're slaves to minding other people's business and to judging it harshly.

Everyone says they hate gossip. Everyone claims not to engage in it. But everyone reading this book knows that these claims are self-serving and often dishonest. Most of us gossip, from priests to little old ladies walking their Yorkshire terriers and little old men playing chess in the park. But when gossip crosses over into slander (malicious, ill-intentioned gossip perpetrated to destroy another's reputation), you're not that far from the evil spirits we were just talking about in the last chapter.

And that kind of nastiness need not be tolerated, especially when you have tools at your disposal to deal with it.

So, let's figure out why people wag their tongues, to begin with. *What's their problem?*

Why Do People Gossip and Slander?

As I stated above, we all do it to a certain degree. Some people gossip as a way of life. It's their entertainment, their comfort, their connection to other people. It's probably an international sport, in some twisted way.

Gossip is bad enough, even when the gossip is only mildly offensive. But the slander is another matter. For example, "Oh, it looks like (insert name) gained back all that weight he/she lost!" or "My God, did you hear she's leaving her husband for another man?" Other people's weight, other aspects of their appearance, financial situation, and sex lives are the usual topics of conversation when gossip convene.

But when that gossip becomes malicious and people say things like, "That person is really dishonest," or "That person is a known philanderer," or "See that guy – don't give him any encouragement. He will screw you out of everything." There may be some arcane grain of truth, but it's clear that the intention behind such words is to discredit the person in question socially and as much as possible on a wider field.

And that is slander. When we say things that we're not sure are true but have been passed through the slimy entrails of the gossip mill, we are engaging in slander. Slander can ruin lives and reputations. It can tear relationships apart (which is quite often the whole point of the malicious chatter involved).

People, despite all the thrilling events happening in our modern world, are bored. They feel they're not part of the great spectacle of life. For this reason and reasons of envy, jealousy, and just ill-temper, the gossips and slanderers of this world engage in creating clouds of animus that are often based on nothing and which have the power to destroy lives.

But why would people gossip about you, much less slander you? What have you done to deserve that?

Targets of gossips and slanderers are usually:

- Well-liked
- Kind
- Decent
- Happy
- Attractive
- Reasonably well off (and even if they're not, they *think* they are because they're not obsessed with material things)

In other words, it's almost always the blameless and decent who fall to the acid tongues of gossip and slander. Something about a person who has their ducks happily in a row, minding their business and doing their thing, sets off the envy together with its friend with the green eyes, in people. That's because most people are not well-liked, kind, decent, happy, attractive, and content with their financial circumstances. They look at the object of their chatter with jaundiced eyes, suspecting that this annoyingly whole and well specimen must have dark secrets.

They're asking themselves, *"Why don't I have that? Why am I not like that person? Why does that person have everything? That should be me!"*

Rotten, isn't it? You just mind your business, and BAM, some of that gossip (and woefully) slander goes around the mulberry bush until someone decides they should tell you what's being said. You're blindsided and sideswiped. You've been nothing but pleasant. In fact, you weren't even worried about gossip and slander because you thought you gave people no reason to stab you in the back that way.

Think again.

The more pleasant and desirable attributes you claim, the more likely it is that you'll find your name in the mouths of people who dirty it.

So, let's talk about what we can do when these loose-lipped, poison-tongued haters say things they can't take back.

Slapping Down the Haters

As I've said throughout this book, casting is not a tool to be used to exact revenge. It's there to help you and to stop negative energy, entities, and people from messing with your mojo. Always remember the backbone of Wicca – and any worthy system of thought, action, and belief – "an do ye no harm." This is the guiding principle for all we do when we call on the elements for protection, wellbeing, and tranquility in our lives.

Haters are going to hate, as they say. You can't stop that. You can stop them directing their hate at you in the form of gossip and slander. The following spells are all the protection spells you'll need to slap down the haters.

Candle Spell

You'll need:

- Five white candles
- Extra virgin oil
- A sharp implement for carving

Here's what you need to do:

1. Place the items on your altar and cast your circle.

2. On one of these candles, you'll carve your name, focusing your intention on protection from malicious gossip or slander circulating.

3. Now, anoint all five candles with olive oil.

4. Place the candle with your name carved into it in the center of the altar.

5. Around that central candle, place the other four candles at the cardinal directors – north, south, east, and west. As you do, acknowledge the four directions and the elements they represent (see Chapter 3).

6. Lighting the central candle, say something like, "This candle represents me, the object of malicious chatter by (insert name of gossiper), whose heart is full of lies and slander. (Gossipers) intentions are malevolent when I have done nothing wrong. I stand in honesty and purity, asking that this malicious chatter will cease."

7. Now, light the candle to the west and say something like, "I walk in truth. Lies cannot stick to me."

8. Light the candle to the north, saying words to the effect of, "Truth is my guide."

9. Light the candle to the east, saying something like, "With truth as my guide, my enemies cannot draw near."

10. Light the final candle to the south, saying words to the effect of, "I stand on truth and purity."

11. As the candles burn, contemplate truth and purity as your friends, enveloping you with their best to protect you from harm. Meditate on this imagery and envision the gossiper as standing outside the protective embrace of truth and purity for no less than 10 minutes.

When you're satisfied that you've spent enough time in contemplation honoring the spell, snuff the candles out (instead of blowing them out). This ritual may be performed every three days until you sense that the hater has been slapped down.

Sweet Solution

You'll need:

- A paper and pen
- A glass
- A small amount of water (separate from the glass)
- Pure cane sugar

Here's what to do:

1. Place the items on your altar and cast your circle.

2. Fill your glass with a cup of water, adding one tablespoon of the cane sugar, and stir gently as you focus on the sweetness of the truth.

3. Now, write the gossip's name with the pen on the piece of paper with the intention in mind that their tongue will be stilled. Place this in the glass of sugar water. Place the glass on a sunny windowsill in your home and leave it there, undisturbed for a week. As you do, contemplate on the sweetness of the sugar, and the sun's revealing light.

The purifying rays of the sun and the sweetness of the sugar will work together to purify the negative influence of gossip. And you may find that people start to see that the gossip is a liar. Nothing can hide from the sun.

Freezing Spell

You'll need:

- A freezer bag
- A sheet of paper and a black pen
- A small amount of water

Here's what to do:

1. Place these items on your altar and cast your circle.

2. Writer the hater's name on the sheet of paper with the black pen, focusing on the intention that this person will be frozen where they stand, no longer slandering you.

3. Fill the freezer bag halfway with water.

4. Put it in the freezer and leave it there as you contemplate the mouth of your hater being "frozen."

As always, every action you take must be accompanied by a powerful intention. You can visualize the gossip's mouth unable to open until it no longer slanders you.

Spell to Change the Game

You'll need:

- An indigo candle (the color is directed related to sopping malicious chatter)
- A sharp implement for carving
- Extra virgin olive oil
- Protective herbs (see Chapter 4)

Here's how to cast the spell:

1. Place all these tools on your altar and cast the circle. (NB: As the candle needs to burn all the way down for this spell, plan your time for this circle. You may use the time to cast, contemplate, meditate, or even read literature related to the spells you perform in the circle).

2. With focused intention, carve the words "Chattering haters" into the indigo candle.

3. Next, anoint the candle with olive oil and protection herbs.

Light the candle as you ask the spirits to surround you with protection and goodwill. Remain in the circle until the candle has burned down, as every moment you cast in the circle and contemplate your work, you gather power. This will invest your spell with greater power.

Get My Name Out of Your Mouth!

Here's what you will need:

- A piece of toilet tissue
- A black marker
- A pair of scissors

Here's one I'm not going to tell you to cast a circle for - unless you're into casting in the bathroom. For, you will require a toilet! *Yes! A toilet.*

Instead, an act of self-blessing will empower you to cast. Structure it something like this:

1. Envision silver light flooding around you.

2. Now envision golden light flooding you as you take three deep breaths.

3. Next, envision white light filling your every cell with its blinding presence. These three lights unite the moon, sun, and force of all the love the universe consists of.

4. Now, bless yourself. Bless your feet taking you on a sacred journey. Bless your knees that kneel before the altar. Bless your heart, beating in the beauty of love. Bless your lips that partner with the five elements.

5. Following your self-blessing, spread your arms wide to the universe's love and protection, pulling it toward you as a sign that you have accepted these sacred gifts. Then say:

"By my will, so mote it be." *Now carry on!*

This simple little spell is for anyone who can't take another minute of rumors and gossip. And while it will make you giggle, it will also have the effect of turning the gossiper's head. What's more, there is nothing more purifying than laughter, and laughing gayly as you perform this spell makes it even more powerful.

6. Draw a set of lips in the center of your piece of toilet tissue. As you do so, your intention is toward the gossiper, and you may say, "Get my name out of your mouth and keep it out!"

7. Next, write your name. Then, write the gossiper's name.

8. Write the statements being made by the gossiper around the edges of the paper as you stand in front of the toilet. Contemplate the issues these statements represent for you.

9. Now, cut your name out of the toilet tissue with the scissors.

10. Now, throw the remainder of the piece of toilet tissue into the toilet.

11. As you flush the inscribed toilet tissue away, say the name of the gossiper and again tell them to get your name out of their mouth and keep it out. Then loudly state, "Your name is banished! Mine is unblemished!"

12. Smile as you merrily flush your hater's name down the toilet.

Gaelic Anti-Gossip Spell

You'll need:

- Powdered clove
- A piece of white paper and a red pen
- A red candle

Cast the spell like this:

1. Place all these items on your altar and cast your circle.

2. Write the gossiper's name backward with the red pen. You may then write an admonition against the gossiper's attacks on you, like, "The chatter will now cease!"

3. At 7 AM and 7 PM each day, you will cast your circle and light the red candle. You will perform this ritual for seven days. As you light the candle, sprinkle a little of the powdered clove into the candle's flame while at the same time, you're focusing your intention on the cessation of gossip by the person responsible. When your ritual is completed each time, snuff out the candle.

4. On the seventh day after lighting the 7 PM candle (which is the final lighting of the candle for this ritual), place the remainder of your powdered clove into the piece of paper on which you wrote the gossiper's name backward. Burn paper and clove together.

Gossip and slander are part of the human condition. We all participate in our own ways, but most of us don't wish ill on others as we do so. We're just sharing information about other people without ill intent. Humans are curious creatures. We want to know what people are up to, if they're happy, or need some help that we might be able to give. We're social creatures, so sharing innocuous tidbits about friends we have in common with others is part of how we live out that social impulse. Our knowledge of those we spend time with binds us to them and increases our intimacy with them.

But that's different from gossip and slander. These ways of talking about others are not intended to bind together but to tear apart, defame, and cast doubt.

And remember, friends, that when people talk about you, it's usually because you're interesting or stand out in some other way. Be proud of who you are but never be arrogant. We're all just feeble humans walking each other home, and as we walk together, the way is so much more pleasant when we walk in goodwill and not the toxic cloud of gossip and slander.

Be aware, always, of the energies of those around you. You're probably thinking a lot more about it since you started reading this book, aren't you? That's a good thing! Because energetic awareness is the beginning of learning to protect yourself. Reading the energies around you is like getting an early warning system for potential problems with petty people.

Never ignore a red flag. Never give people the benefit of the doubt, but do test those perceptions against your observations. Be honest. We are truthful. Stand in purity and, while protecting yourself and others, refuse to be taken in by the wayward words of the unworthy.

Next, we're going to talk about protecting the people you love with protection spells and how to prepare yourself and those beloved people for your casting work.

Chapter Eleven: Protecting Your Loved Ones

We all deeply desire that our loved ones be kept safe from all harm. Sometimes, we can't do anything to help, or at least it feels that way.

But being proactive about keeping those around us safe is always a good policy, which is where protection spells for saving your loved ones from harm come in.

That said, there are some important points to know, remember and consider before you throw yourself at the project, *as I know you're all dying to!*

Don't Be a Sticky Beak (a prying person)

We've talked about obsession and burnout earlier in this book. That's a major part of the problem with being a sticky beak. Your obsession with your new focus in life will probably be so exciting to you that you want to share it with everyone you know!

Whether they're interested or not.

And that's a very important point to ponder on. Some will not be even remotely receptive to the idea of casting. Some will be ignorant and have popular fantasies in their minds which don't apply. The message is clear – know when you're being a pain.

In addition, never cast on behalf of someone who doesn't know what you're up to. The loved one you're trying to protect may not desire or want your intervention. They may have certain convictions which preclude any magical intervention on your part, even if that intervention is as benign as everything else offered in this book.

The urge to help others can sometimes overwhelm our understanding of our place in people's lives. For example, you may not like the new boyfriend or girlfriend of a friend. You may have detected unpleasant energies emanating from this person. While it's tempting just to blurt it out and offer your friend protection, it's much more effective to acknowledge the energies, observe the behavior and find an opening. While it's hard to wait, you'll have more information and a leg to stand on.

Don't rush in where angels fear to tread, for you are not a fool!

In addition, it's always good to know a little about the history of the person on whose behalf you're casting. Once you have their permission, put out tentative feelers to see if you can pick up on any bad blood that might be lurking in their past. Is someone holding a grudge? Is your loved one aware of any curses that might need to be lifted (for these can get in the way of any protective castings you perform on their behalf, especially if the curse is generational)?

Remember that awareness and openness are definitely required in any protection spell you're offering to your loved ones.

Prepare

Once you have permission from a loved one to cast a protection spell and have talked to them about potential roadblocks like curses and such, you can begin your preparations for casting.

Because the protection spell you'll be casting is intended to protect someone other than yourself, you must think about what you're doing and draft a plan. This plan is spiritual and will protect both you and the person you're casting on behalf of.

Here's a template for proceeding:

- Distill the goal for your protection spell down to a guiding thought. For instance – "I will protect my loved ones from negative energies by casting a protective veil around them.
- Consider how your protection spell will impact others. Think of the butterfly or ripple effect.
- Ensure you have the right kind of positive support and reinforcement around you.
- Be convicted in your action and positive in your energy. Be who you say you are.

This simple framework keeps you focused on the work at hand and the reason you're doing it. It prevents spiritual confusion and negativity from impacting your personal energies by being clear and intentional about the protection spell you'll be casting. Also, you need the support of others as much as you need the protection circle. Their positive and loving intentions toward you are fortifying and enriching.

Once you're prepared, you're confident and powerful. You've done the necessary preparation, having modeled the patience you need to be an effective ally to your loved ones, as one who actively seeks their wellbeing. Already, your intention is lovingly noble. When you add confidence and power to the loving, noble intention, you have a force of nature.

Being prepared means being aware that by choosing to cast on behalf of your loved ones, you're declaring your right to exist peacefully. It's your life, and you will control it. Not everyone will accept that, but they're not the people that matter, so don't mind them.

Go into all protection spells (particularly this one, as there is personal responsibility involved), resolving and intending to think clearly, act justly, and cast humbly. And remember that once a spell is cast, you need to forget it! Let it do its job without obsessing about it. Don't forget to explain this to the loved one or loved ones you're casting for.

Calling on the God Janus

You'll need:

- A stick of butter
- Coffee (about ½ a cup)
- The names of those you're protecting your loved one from (alternatively, the energies or institutions that are threatening them) written in black pen.
- A coffee filter
- A bowl

For this spell – like the toilet spell – we will forego the casting circle and use the self-blessing described in Chapter 10: Get my name out your mouth.

You'll be casting with fire for this one, using your cooking top as part of your protection spell.

Janus is the Roman god with two faces looking in opposite directions. For the Romans, Janus was the god of all new beginnings. Wherever something is about to be born or is initiated, there is the two-faced god.

Here's what we're going to do:

- Place the coffee filter in the bowl. Before doing so, you will have written the rune or symbol of Janus on the filter. Alternatively, you'll simply write the god's name.
- Now, add the butter, heating it together with the filter.
- Next, place the paper with the name of the person, people, institution, or energies you're trying to protect your loved one from.

• Respectfully and humbly request Janus's assistance in removing the interest of the party or parties involved, neutralizing their influence in your loved ones' life through God's intervention.

When you've completed the spell and given thanks for being granted the assistance of Janus, make sure the contents of the bowl are disposed of properly. Wrap the spell's ingredients tightly and dispose of it far from your home, burning the package if possible.

This spell is exceedingly simple and great for beginners, with the right energetic output and intention. It's also an extraordinarily potent and effective protection spell. It can be adapted to protect you, an individual, or a group of people. Janus's mission is successful fresh starts, so invoking the assistance of this god is one of the best casting decisions you can make – especially for those you seek to protect.

To Protect Your Pets

Pets bring another dimension of love and presence to our lives. I believe that animals are perfect creatures. They only scheme and strategize to hunt. Despite our tendency toward anthropomorphism, animals bear none of our deceptions. They are simply and peacefully who they are. And while animals have a certain type of sentience, they have no concept of death – the source of so many human neuroses.

In short, animals are *da' bomb* and deserve all the love, attention, and protection we can give them.

So, let's cast for our little, furry buddies!

You'll need:

- A brown candle
- A glass of water
- A photo of your pet. Alternatively, write the name of your pet down.
- An image or prayer card of St. Francis, Patron of Animals (or maybe your local animal rescue hero, if you prefer).
- A pair of scissors

And here's how to do it:

1. Put the required articles on your altar, except for the photo or written name of your pet and the prayer card or image of your animal rescue hero. Leave those nearby.

2. Cast your circle.

3. Put your pet's photo (or name, written down) on the altar in between the water and the candle.

4. Now, take the prayer card image of St. Francis (or your alternative) and saying something to the effect of:

"I come to ask for protection for my dear (pet's name). This is the friend I share my days with. I love (pet's name) and pledge to care for him/her as the universe cares for us all. I beg that should (pet's name) be lost, that he return to me; that should (pet's name) be injured or ill, that he/she be healed."

5. Now, sprinkle a little water on the photo of your pet or the name of your pet.

6. Give thanks to St. Francis (or your alternative) for his intervention.

7. Allow the candle to continue burning, then snuff it out.

8. The tip of the candle should be cut off with scissors. You may now conclude your circle, but your spell is not yet complete.

9. The tip of the candle should be buried with the photo somewhere on your property. If you have no outdoor property, bury this in a planter (vertically is fine).

10. Don't forget to dispose of the water in any way you choose.

Most people put bells on their cats to keep them from killing birds and other small wild animals by hopefully frightening the intended prey off. But the addition of a bell to the collar of any pet (cat, dog, guinea pig, ferret) has the effect of not only keeping birds and small animals out of harm's way but negativity, too. This is another great way to protect your pet (and all the little woodland creatures while you're at it).

Keep negativity in the home to the bare minimum, as animals instantly pick up on it and absorb it. They can also sense negative energy, so they act as harbingers of the undesirable.

In our next and final chapter, we're going to talk about a few regularly practiced protection rituals keyed to the moon. The moon and its influence is a discussion that has filled thousands of books, but this chapter will serve as a brief introduction.

Chapter Twelve: Daily and Monthly Protection

I would be remiss if I were to leave you without a brief discussion about the moon. It's important to understand how the moon affects us, how it guides time, and how it's so much more than just a light high in the sky. Days are divided from one another by the moon, and the month represents one full cycle of the moon.

The moon has a powerful influence on all life. Because the human body is made primarily of water – like all living things -human life responds just as powerfully to the moon's cycles as does all other life.

But many of us are almost completely unconscious of the moon's influence on our psychological settings and behaviors. Of course, the word "lunacy" is derived from the Latin word "Luna," meaning moon.

But the moon influences all waterlogged life forms. And that has an environmental impact. Like the seasons of the sun, the moon's cyclical incarnations control the tides, and the tides define the edges of our physical existence. As the oceans move with the lunar cycle, so do human bodies and human psychology, of course, follows.

The watery human body rolls with lunar cycles to such a large degree that all three of the Great Near Eastern Monotheistic faiths follow the moon in determining the arrival of festivals like Easter, Pesach (Passover), and Ramadan. But the moon's influence even affects the organization of human time, counted in months according to the behaviors of our pale accomplice in the sky.

And because we're talking about protection spells, we need to talk a little bit about how the moon affects casting. And yes, of course, it does. Human hands, minds, and spirits are doing the casting!

The Phases of the Moon

Each month, the moon passes through eight distinct phases. *As you read, picture the moon's phases described arranged in a circle, starting at the top and moving clockwise.*

- First quarter
- Waxing crescent
- New moon
- Waning crescent
- Last quarter
- Waning gibbous
- Full moon

The most crucial phases for our purposes are five, specifically:

- New moon
- Full moon
- Crescent moon
- Waning moon
- Waxing moon

In terms of spells, the new moon is chosen by practitioners whenever a new beginning is necessary. The full moon is an optimal time to build power. The crescent moon is a modest time of building. The waxing moon is an ambitious time of building, and the waning moon is time to revise plans that haven't worked out or changed.

I know these are all drearily general descriptions, but your knowledge base is only beginning its journey with this book. Your curiosity and interest will grow from here. But understanding what the phases of the moon are inviting practitioners to do at certain times is another tool in your arsenal. Your reverence and attention are appreciated because the moon so potently defines humanity's intimate connection to the natural world.

The moon has many gifts for you. Your gift to the moon is to appreciate its glorious role in this human life. Understanding the benefit of your casting and its intentions is your intentional interaction with the moon and another way of bringing peace to the universe.

Regularly Scheduled Protection

You're learning as much about yourself, most likely, as you are about protective magic. As your knowledge of how protection spells work and how you relate to them grows, you'll have much more freedom to develop your own rituals, drawing on the practice of those who've gone before. And that increasing depth in self-knowledge is so desirable on many levels.

Your sense of connection with the work you're doing is a prime determinant of the success of your casting. That's very important and necessary. But there is a sacred foundation for that work that demands acknowledgment if not necessarily dogmatically prescribed.

Your acknowledgment and understanding of the matrix of elemental power interacting with a human agency is really what all this protection magic business is about.

Because it's the individual and the individual's body, mind, and spirit which are at the center of working protection magic, your relationship to the elements and to the natural world is where the true power of your work resides.

And as we discussed earlier, the individual conscience of the practitioner is guided by the core tenet of Wicca: "an do ye no harm." On this hangs all else.

Even the Law of Three is intimately guided by the warning and spirit of not to do harm. You cannot understand the Law of Three without understanding that doing harm snaps back on you. This is one of Wicca's few non-negotiables. Spells and even materials are subject to the practitioner's relationship with the elements. Don't forget that the fifth element is spirit, in which two types of consciousness interact. That is not to say that the other elements are inanimate, either. They are just animated in a different way.

All the elements cry out for a relationship with us to bring about greater universal tranquility and wellbeing. Tranquility and wellbeing are for the five living, breathing elements as much as they are for us.

So, with profound joy, find in these suggestions about regular rituals a grounding for growing yourself into a greater relationship with the elements and the natural world they reveal to you. Know that the ground you stand on is sacred because it is the wellspring of all life, joy, and love.

Why Regular Rituals?

You'll recall that you shouldn't hang on to your spells. Part of that is to please the element of spirit. Obsessing about spells once they've been cast is a little disrespectful to those we don't see. It's like not trusting the process, and that's a short, easy road to nowhere. *Disrespected spirits are unhappy spirits.*

Another reason we don't hang onto spells is that it expresses a certain lack of confidence on the practitioner's part. Then why bother with all this? It seems a rather hollow exercise if you haven't acknowledged your role in the great drama of the universe. Part of developing your confidence as a practitioner is to know that your relationship with the natural world is healthy. In that health is your ability to let go of spells, once cast.

Daily and monthly rituals ground you in your practice - another great confidence booster. As your practice evolves, you'll find specific areas of focus that emerge naturally in your life. Because we're talking about protection spells in this book, that's what our ritual focus will be. Just be aware that all are adaptable and that all is ultimately determined, in spirit, by you.

Moon Protection Ritual

You'll need:

- White candle
- A small sheet of white paper
- Blue pen
- The name of the planet associated with your zodiac sign and the names of its moons

On rising each day, acknowledge the moon as a protective presence is a powerful ritual. In this one, the moon is entreated to envelop you with its protective power.

For this morning ritual, you may either cast a circle or say a self-affirmation (see Chapter 10, "Get my name out your mouth"), whichever you choose. You are invoking protection from the moon as a daily homage and protection spell. If you feel you require the protection of the circle, so be it.

Here's how it goes:

1. Write your zodiac sign on one side of the sheet of paper. On the other side, write the name of the planet associated with your sign.

2. Next, light the candle, chanting the names of the moons of the planet associated with your zodiac sign. After you chant these, chant your middle name. Continue chanting the names of the moons and your middle name after these.

3. Now, you will burn the sheet of paper using the candle's flame. Carry on chanting until the flames have died down.

4. Once the paper has burned – but while the candle is still lit – imagine the room transforming to become flooded with your favorite color. Gaze at the candle, enjoying its dance. Allow yourself to bask in its warmth and the joyful color all around you.

Invoking the moon each morning for your protection is both a self-empowering action and one which honors the moon's place in our lives. In this relationship, you are both protected and connected.

Evening Prayer to Protect the Mind and Spirit

You'll need:

- Protection herb oil
- Natural incense (copal or frankincense)

The night can be a time of danger for those who walk this earth unprotected. This evening ritual will protect your mind from unwanted "reading" on the part of those hoping to control you. It will also protect you from the influence of evil tendencies around you or aware of you and hoping to cause trouble.

Of course, self-affirm before speaking this prayer. Casting a circle is, in this instance, up to you. Light your natural incense and anoint yourself with your chosen protective oil, then proceed.

This is a prayer, not a ritual and speaking it with intention is the entire spell. But if you speak this prayer using the words you prefer, your intention increases.

"Tonight, as every night, those who stand guard over all secrets hold in their hands my heart. That my mind and spirit's doors be locked and inviolable."

Weekly Rituals

To veil yourself with protection, the regular schedule rituals you're learning about continue the requests you offered in specific protection spells, reinforcing them with your actions. Holding the thought – that you need and desire protection – can be subsumed by life's constant needs. Scheduling a ritual that you do each week to satisfy your ongoing requests and intentions for protection serves to undergird all past and future ritual work.

Ritual Protective Bath

You'll need:

- A stream, river, pond, lake, or the sea (if not possible, a bath at home will do, with the right intentions and maybe rather a lot of sea salt)
- Oil of clove (for anointing)
- Sage smudge
- Natural incense (copal is very connected to water, especially in aboriginal cultures in Latin America)
- Salt
- Black salt

Bathing is a commonly used type of ritual, existing in many cultures. The Christian baptism, adapted from the Jewish mikveh, is one of the most widely known ritual baths.

Earlier in this book, we discussed a bath for the removal of a hex. Here, we'll talk about how you can create your ritual protective bath, drawing on your ritual tools and knowledge.

You'll need a quiet, little-frequented spot for this ritual. Remember that you don't want to be interrupted, disrupting the energies around you and your ritual bath.

This ritual protection bath is mostly for you to create. Think about the type of protection you need and why you need it. And remember that purifying yourself before ritually bathing is a step that must be taken. This is a ritual to protect you from external sources of negativity, not anything you're self-generating.

So, before engaging in the ritual as you've planned it, be sure to anoint yourself with protective oil of clove, asking that its purifying essence prepare you for the ritual bath. As you smudge yourself, keep the same intention in mind, ensuring you're ready for ritual. Proceed with self-affirmation when you've done this, as described in Chapter 10 (according to your preferences).

When you've done this, light your incense in a ceremonial vessel or as a stick, planted in the natural earth, moss, dirt, or sand, next to your water source. You may remain clothed as this is a ritual bath. You're there to gird yourself with powerful, protective energy, not wash behind your ears!

Write the symbol you most passionately connect within the air (see Chapter Five), structuring your intentions to include invoking this ancient symbol's protective powers. Now, with the salt, bless the ground as you seek the loving protection of all the elements.

With the black salt, anoint yourself, as you say words like, "The living waters I come to bathe in are the same as my mother's womb, where once I was safest. I humbly request the warmth and protection of the living waters against all harm."

Performing the ritual bath as a weekly experience may be a challenge in some climates but be creative. And if you can't find a natural source of water you can bathe in, bathe at home. What matters most about rituals like these is not where you're bathing but your intention and your intimate connection to the elements you're partnering with.

PRO-TIP: If bathing at home, allow the hot water to melt the salt intended for your bathing ritual and then sprinkle black salt over the top of the bath when running it. You may also pour some of your clove oil in the bath or oil made with another protective herb, as described in Chapter Four, instead of anointing yourself.

Next, I'd like you to encourage your growth. You're learning about the roles of protective tools and how to use them, so now it's time to get practical with that knowledge. For this final part of our exploration of protection spells, you'll create your own rituals based on the two most iconic phases of the moon (new and full).

Relax, reach out to the cosmos, cast your circle, and get ready to become a co-creator.

New Moon Protection Ritual

When the moon is new, it is perfectly aligned in the heavens with the sun, so we don't see it. The cycle of the moon's phases has concluded; the new moon stands as a tabula rasa (blank slate), waxing again through its phases to its delightful fullness.

When the moon is not visible to us, we miss it. We realize something profoundly beautiful is absent from our lives. The new moon is a moment of the profound connection between you and the moon as you go inward to reflect in the darkness of your friend's absence.

The basis of creating a ritual is to infuse it with who you are. What are your personal parameters? What are your desires for the ritual? Creating your own rituals is about reaching for your unexpressed desires in any given moment and giving them a voice. You're following no rules, except the only one that matters in your context: "an do ye no harm."

Full Engagement Ritual Creation

The herbs, oils, crystals, amulets, candles, and any other tools you use in your rituals are there to do a job, but they're also there to ground you in the ritual. They have a purpose beyond mere sensuality or their respective roles.

The intimacy of and engagement with the ritual invests it with the power you're trying to evoke. Intention forms another layer of the kind of intimacy and engagement we're talking about. Every part of you is alive with the work as you engage with the objects and substances you've brought to it.

Much of what you require to create a ritual is already in place. What's now needed is your full submission to the wonder of the new moon and what it means to you.

Invest some time into thinking about the new moon, how it manifests and what sign it occurs in each month. Do this to locate the element and the corresponding cardinal direction to focus on in your ritual. This adds another layer of focus which some will find enriching, but it's not 100% necessary. (NB: this action is more important for the full moon due to the power of the phase).

You will know what to bring to your sacred protection circle once you've entered the new moon's mysterious precincts. You will have formed a bond with the new moon already and should be conceptualizing it in a completely different way.

As you create your new moon protection ritual, remember that your intention is two-fold. You are giving homage to the new moon and building your mutual bond. You're also petitioning for protection for the coming cycle.

Spare and post-modern or byzantine in complexity – the ritual is yours and yours alone. Precisely the same is true of the full moon, with some minor changes in your thinking around the ritual you're creating to reflect the most iconic lunar phase.

Full Moon Protection Ritual

When the moon is ripe and bright, it sits precisely opposite the sun in the heavens. During this phase, the brightness of the moon is a reflection of the sun's splendid radiance.

That reflection creates groundswells of emotion, drama, turbulence, and excitement. Madness increases, dogs' bay, and cats luxuriate in the glow of the full moon's glory.

What does the full moon do (*and it does "do," doesn't it?*) to you? You may feel like dancing or finding someone to dance with. Perhaps you feel emotionally or spiritually abundant. Some fire on all cylinders at the full moon. Others misfire. The way you personally respond to the full moon is the basis for your full moon protection ritual.

Again, remember that your purpose here is two-fold. On the one hand, you desire to bring honor to the moon in its most heartbreakingly glorious phase. On the other, you're petitioning for the protection of this ravishing creature. These thoughts combine to guide you toward the full moon ritual, which most abundantly expresses your physical, intellectual, and spiritual responses to the phase. And don't forget to look up the sign the moon has waxed full in. The power of this celestial body in its full phase demands that you do. Add a symbol of the sign's element (air, air, fire, water) to your altar.

The full moon is a symbol of mystery and romance. Remember the movie, *Moonstruck?* Hold that thought. The potency of the full moon cannot be denied in its effects on we mere mortals. Work with that potency. Work with your own potency, grown within the protective bounds of your sacred circle.

Connect with the full moon only in the most naked truth. Be clear. Before you perform this ritual, cleanse your energy with sage or with a ritual bath. That is my best advice, as you're about to make a powerful friend on the full moon.

Now, journey on, celebrating the protection spell caster you're becoming. Here is where we must part.

Do ye no harm. Blessed be!

Conclusion

It has been my great honor to share the contents of this book with you. I hope I've made it clear that casting protection spells is something anyone can do to bring greater peace, tranquility, and wellbeing to their lives.

Always remember that magic is everywhere and for everyone. There is no dividing line between the practitioner and the elements. There is only direct communion without mediating influence or hierarchy. This is great freedom.

And wasn't it Spiderman's uncle who warned that with great freedom comes great responsibility? That's as true of having arachnid superpowers as it is of being in communion with the elements.

And so, the Wiccan way teaches to do no harm. This is not a suggestion. It is the backbone of the work and the moral compass of all who come to the elements in casting. Be aware of your intentions, maintain a clear energetic vibration, and do ye no harm to truly walk in the way of elemental enlightenment and the profound sense of spiritual connection that doing so imparts.

Here's another book by Mari Silva that you might like

Your Free Gift (only available for a limited time)

Thanks for getting this book! If you want to learn more about various spirituality topics, then join Mari Silva's community and get a free guided meditation MP3 for awakening your third eye. This guided meditation mp3 is designed to open and strengthen ones third eye so you can experience a higher state of consciousness. Simply visit the link below the image to get started.

https://spiritualityspot.com/meditation

References

Anti-slander spell - protection from torment and slander. (n.d.). Everythingunderthemoon.Net. Retrieved from https://everythingunderthemoon.net/spells/anti-slander-spell.htm

Author, M. F. T. (n.d.). *Psychic attack – how to build up effective psychic shielding: New age movement.* Newagemovement.Org. Retrieved from https://newagemovement.org/psychic-attack/

Caro, T. (2019, April 16). *5 free Protection Spells for loved ones [protection magic].* Magickalspot.Com. https://magickalspot.com/protection-spells-guide/

Caro, T. (2020, June 14). *4 potent essential oils for Spiritual Protection [& usages].* Magickalspot.Com. https://magickalspot.com/spiritual-protection-essential-oils/

Dylan, Anna, Anonymous, Rabhen, Wayne, Bntru2me, Fields, K., AJP, Alice, A., Tony, Jake, T, Koch, J. L., James, Guest, Davis, W., ANONYMOUS, B, Guide, A., ... Randy. (2019, July 10). *15 signs of a curse: Are you really cursed? + how to BREAK A curse!* Otherworldlyoracle.Com. https://otherworldlyoracle.com/signs-curse-breaking-curses/

Five signs that you have been hexed. (n.d.). Originalbotanica.Com. Retrieved from https://www.originalbotanica.com/blog/signs-been-hexed-cursed-black-magic/

Guardian staff reporter. (2003, July 5). Can a guru heal himself? *The Guardian.* http://www.theguardian.com/books/2003/jul/05/booksonhealth.lifeand health

Kyteler, E. (2021, January 10). *How to make A protection jar (ingredients & spell).* Eclecticwitchcraft.Com. https://eclecticwitchcraft.com/how-to-make-a-protection-jar-ingredients-spell/

Lunar protection spell: Super easy full moon ritual. (2018, November 9). Spells8.Com. https://spells8.com/lunar-protection-spell/

Pagans, 3., & Cat, A. (2020, May 12). *Protection magick: Why and how it is useful in everyday life.* Patheos.Com. https://www.patheos.com/blogs/3pagansandacat/2020/05/protection-spells-why-and-how-it-is-useful-in-everyday-life/

Pfeifle, T. (2020, April 21). *Apotropaic Magic.* Astonishinglegends.Com; Astonishing Legends. https://www.astonishinglegends.com/astonishing-legends/2020/4/21/apotropaic-magic

Pollux, A. (2019, October 30). 12 powerful herbs for protection to keep you safe and stong. *Wiccanow.Com.* https://wiccanow.com/herbs-for-protection/

Rice, J. (2014, February 15). *Plants that repel evil spirits & demons.* Ghostlyactivities.Com. https://www.ghostlyactivities.com/plants-repel-evil-spirits-demons/

The Moonlight Shop. (n.d.). *5 Wiccan symbols for protection you should be using now.* Themoonlightshop.Com. Retrieved from https://themoonlightshop.com/blogs/news/5-wiccan-symbols-for-protection-you-should-be-using-now

Wigington, P. (n.d.). *Protection Magic.* Learnreligions.Com. Retrieved from https://www.learnreligions.com/magic-protection-spells-and-rituals-2562176

(N.d.). Washingtonpost.Com. Retrieved from https://www.washingtonpost.com/posteverything/wp/2016/07/01/as-a-psychiatrist-i-diagnose-mental-illness-and-sometimes-demonic-possession/

Printed in Great Britain
by Amazon

80998036R00071